A Play On Words

Also by Deric Longden

DIANA'S STORY
LOST FOR WORDS
THE CAT WHO CAME IN FROM THE COLD
I'M A STRANGER HERE MYSELF
ENOUGH TO MAKE A CAT LAUGH

A Play On Words

Deric Longden

BANTAM PRESS

LONDON · NEW YORK · TORONTO · SYDNEY · AUCKLAND

TRANSWORLD PUBLISHERS
61–63 Uxbridge Road, London W5 5SA
a division of The Random House Group Ltd

RANDOM HOUSE AUSTRALIA (PTY) LTD
20 Alfred Street, Milsons Point, Sydney,
New South Wales 2061, Australia

RANDOM HOUSE NEW ZEALAND LTD
18 Poland Road, Glenfield, Auckland 10, New Zealand

RANDOM HOUSE (PTY) LTD
Endulini, 5A Jubilee Road, Parktown 2193, South Africa

Published 1999 by Bantam Press
a division of Transworld Publishers

A catalogue record for this book is available from
the British Library
ISBN 0593 044029

Typeset in 11½/14pt Times by Kestrel Data, Exeter, Devon.

Printed in Great Britain by
Clays Ltd, Bungay, Suffolk.

3 5 7 9 10 8 6 4 2

A Play On Words

Chapter One

My eyes snapped shut as I pulled open the thick study curtains, the bright morning light etching its way in through my lids. Hardly had any sleep again last night. I could kill those damn birds.

There are two of them, a tall one and a short one, and they sit on the chimney stack, by the skylight, and wake me with a start at twenty-two minutes past four every blessed morning. The tall one is into light opera and performs highlights from *The Desert Song* and *Madam Butterfly*, while the short one is a throwback to the old music-hall days. He's brought his act up to date and now specializes in impressions of mobile phones, selections from Nokia and Ericsson, and one day I'm going to wring his bloody neck.

They also have a friend who visits every now and then. His conversation is somewhat limited. He bellows '*Hello, Kevin*' at six-minute intervals, but it must have been his morning off.

The park across the narrow lane from our house was almost empty except for a gardener, armed with a black plastic bin-liner, rounding up the wrappings from last night's fish and chips. The Coke tins had already been spirited away by a freelancer. You can get forty pence a kilo for them down at Alcan, but you have to be up early or they're gone.

From time to time the council have a crackdown on the offending muck-spreaders. They call them litter louts. My neighbour Patrick calls them arseholes and I think Patrick has it by a short head.

An old man eased himself down on the bench two storeys below me. I could see the checkered top of his cloth cap and the narrow spread of his hunched shoulders. He held a cardboard pizza box out at arm's length, distastefully, between finger and thumb, and dropped it in the bin-liner as it floated by.

The door swung open and Aileen staggered into my study. She placed two full bottles of milk on my desk and then, shivering dramatically, pulled her robe tight around her.

'Why is fresh air always so draughty?'

Fresh air changes its mind far too often for her liking. She's basically your centrally heated sort of woman. If she wore a more sensible robe she wouldn't feel the cold half as much. It's nothing more than a wrap of thin cotton with lacy bits you can see right through, totally unsuited to the English climate. I bought it for her.

I peeped in through one of the lacy bits and congratulated myself on my good taste.

'Why do I have two bottles of milk on my desk?'

She was most surprised to see them there and said that she didn't really know. Then she thought about it. As she did so she slumped down in the recliner chair and searched her pockets for a pack of cigarettes.

'I think you'll find there's a small brown-paper parcel for you in the fridge.'

I got up to go and get it. She's always like this in the

morning. Her body goes walkabout while her mind is still having a lie-in.

'It'll be on that shelf in the door. The one where we keep the milk. Take those with you if you're going.'

She pointed to the two bottles of milk and leaned over to steal a cigarette from my packet on the side table. I keep them over there so that they are well out of my way while I'm working. If they were on my desk I would be forever reaching out and taking one. As it is I am forever walking over to the side table.

Those thieves who go around stealing small brown-paper parcels from unattended fridges would have no trouble whatsoever in locating ours, even though we keep the fridge hidden, tucked away behind one of twenty-three identical wooden doors.

There will invariably be a cat sitting staring at the fridge, willing the door to swing wide open. This morning there were three of them, all lined up, doing their level best to remember the PIN number.

'Excuse me.'

They didn't. They never do. They sat with their bums glued to the lino and simply swayed backwards so that the door brushed up against their whiskers as I tugged it open. They made copious notes for future reference.

'*Take this down. Ham on bottom shelf. Garlic sausage on second shelf. Can't see on top shelf, but it smells like chicken. Small, unidentified, brown-paper parcel being spirited away. Follow and report.*'

They followed me upstairs. It's amazing how cats who set off hard on your heels can be sitting there waiting for you when you arrive.

Thermal jumped up on my desk. He spends most

of his working day up there, stretched out under the anglepoise lamp, performing the various duties that come thick and fast when you are acting-unpaid-officer in charge of paper clips.

He keeps them on their toes. If it wasn't for him, he says, the paper clips would just lie there in that little plastic thing doing absolutely nothing all day long. So he keeps them on the move and sees to it that they hardly have a minute to themselves. By five o'clock they are absolutely knackered. I don't know what I would do without him.

Tigger gave the parcel a tentative sniff and then gestured to William who immediately strolled over to offer a second opinion. William sniffed at it. In William's opinion this was a parcel not to be sniffed at and so after nothing more than a perfunctory snuffle he walked away in disgust. I passed it over to Aileen.

'It's addressed to you.'

'I know. I sent for it. But it's for you really.'

The bright blue QVC logo told me that she had ordered it from the shopping channel on television. QVC has changed Aileen's life. With her limited sight she can't make out the jewellery that adorns her own fingers, or even see that which hangs around her neck. Earrings are one of life's great mysteries for her and so she has always relied upon my expert description as we gaze in through the jeweller's window.

'It's a sort of bluey-green stone, with a sort of gold thingy all around it.'

But on the shopping channel they have huge close-ups, and if she puts her nose right up to the screen the pendants and rings are twenty-seven inches across. It's wonderful. She can almost see the lobster-claw fastening on today's special offer and a sharp click on the mute button does away with all that waffle and blather that

10

unfortunately comes along with the pictures. A quick telephone call and she has added yet another item to her collection.

But this one was for me, she said. I tore open the parcel and then eased back the lid of a small brown box. It felt expensive. I looked at the invoice – it was expensive. Aileen inched closer.

'Well?'

'It's a ring.'

'It was on special offer. Let me see.'

She slipped the eternity ring on her finger and it fitted perfectly. I passed her the magnifying glass from my desk.

'It's beautiful, isn't it?'

'Very.'

'I like that.'

She gave me a big kiss and went off to get dressed. At the door she paused and looked back.

'Thank you, love. You must think a lot of me.'

I do, of course, and it would appear that I am also very generous.

I always make myself a large cup of coffee at ten o'clock in the morning. Ten o'clock on the dot. It sets me up for the day. By this time I have already made myself a large cup of coffee at nine twenty-three and another at a quarter to ten, but I wouldn't miss my ten o'clock cup of coffee for anything. It sets me up for the day.

I took it over to the window and looked out at the park. The old man was still there, sitting on the bench. He didn't seem to have moved a muscle since I saw him last. Then his cap swivelled slightly to the left as a young Alsatian came over to have a word with him.

They seemed to be getting on rather well until a shiny black Labrador, chasing a bright red frisbee and not looking where he was going, crashed without ceremony into the Alsatian's rear end.

There was no animosity. The two dogs examined each other closely in order to assess the damage. They made a thorough job of it. They seemed to be enjoying themselves and it was some time before they decided that the matter was probably best left in the hands of their respective insurance companies.

An old man in a cloth cap is no match for a bright red frisbee and so the two dogs lolloped off together across the park, leaving him alone on his bench except for a couple of sparrows who were conducting a mopping-up operation on the grass verge.

He looked rather lost. There's something about a pair of shoulders as seen from a second-storey window that is a dead give-away. Off duty, with nothing to occupy them, they seemed tired and weary. A pair of shoulders who had seen it all and done it all over a period of some eighty-odd years and who now realized that this was as good as it was going to get.

I wished the dogs had hung around and kept him company. I like sparrows, they are gutsy little devils, but if it's conversation you're after, forget it.

I wrote for an hour or more, the time seemed to fly by, and then a very damp cat jumped up on my knee and broke my concentration. I think he might have broken my left testicle as well – I must have it checked.

William doesn't enter a room – he takes it by surprise. He bursts in, having started his run somewhere along the M62. The door flies open and suddenly there's a huge black and white blur scattering papers and sleeping cats and turning hearthrugs into instant hump-backed bridges.

I took him to see the vet not long ago. We were shown into an antiseptic consulting room, white as snow

12

with just a single well-scrubbed table and a freshly sluiced tile floor.

But from the moment I carried William in through the door the room became incredibly untidy. As Mrs Roger turned him upside down to examine his under-carriage I could see her glancing around, thinking, I must have this place done out – it's a disgrace.

It's not that William is a scruffy cat. His white bits are as white as you can get and his black bits glisten like newly polished ebony, but his hair is as fine as silk and the slightest breeze keeps it constantly on the move so that even when he's fast asleep he appears to be either on his way back from somewhere or just about to leave.

I dried him off and then did the same for Thermal. He hadn't been anywhere and was as dry as a bone but he has an equal-time clause built into his contract and he expects me to honour it.

I wondered if I ought to go out and dry off the old man. He had been sheltering under a tree and, now the rain had stopped, was making his way back to the bench. He plucked a tabloid newspaper from inside his jacket, spread it on the wet seat and sat down once more.

Something wasn't right. He'd been there for just over three hours now and I was beginning to worry about him. Perhaps if I went out and took a stroll in the park I might come across him unexpectedly, have a word or two and put my mind at rest.

Seen from my high study window the people in the park look as though they have just stepped out of a painting by Lowry, executed during his little known thick-brush period. They have put on a bit of weight perhaps, but still not enough to spoil the illusion. This, however, was

13

the first time I had met a Lowry figure in the flesh. What there was of it.

His thin fingers shuffled the *Daily Mail* along the bench as I sat down beside him, then he muttered out of the corner of his mouth.

'Bit damp. Here, have shome of thish.'

He offered me the centre spread and I caught a glimpse of a woman who claimed that a famous cosmetic surgeon had gone and given her the wrong nose, and now one of her boobs had collapsed. I plonked my bottom down on top of her. It just wasn't her day.

'Thank you very much.'

We sat in silence for a moment or two. The sparrows were still at it. They were now working on a filled pizza crust and were about to experience a cheese surprise. Then the old man turned and gurned, I suppose you might call it – his mouth moving on rubbery gums, in all directions at once.

'Have you any idea what time it ish?'

I glanced at my watch.

'Just gone half-past twelve. You've been here for three and a half hours.'

He flashed me a questioning look, gums cocked and at the ready but saying nothing.

'I work up there,' I explained, pointing over my shoulder towards my study window. 'I was rather worried. I wondered if you were all right.'

He looked searchingly at me then moved a little closer, whispering so the sparrows wouldn't hear.

'I've been to the dentisht. I had an acshident with my teeth. Dropped my top shet in the shink and they've shent 'em off to Batley to be repaired. They won't have 'em back until five o'clock.'

His gums took some time to settle down after that

little outburst. It must have been the longest sentence they'd ever attempted on their own and they were beginning to feel the strain.

'You can't sit here until five o'clock. It's going to rain again.'

'Have to.'

The sky was black as thunder over Almondbury and it was on its way here any minute now.

'Have you come far?'

I knew I couldn't leave him out here in the park – not for another four hours or so.

'No. I jusht live up Marsh.'

Marsh came out as clear as a bell, the perfect address for a man who has just dropped his top shet in the shink. But it was no more than half a mile away and he saw the look on my face.

'I can't go home. Me and my wife have been married for shixty-three yearsh thish year and in all that time I've never let her shee me without my teeth. And I'm not shtarting now.'

I took him into the lounge and settled him down in front of the television. He was confused by the profusion of remote controls.

'Forget that one – it's for the video. That's the one you want, for channels one through to five and then if you press number six you can use this other one for the satellite channels. All you have to do then is . . .'

But I'd lost him. Thermal had jumped up on his knee and was pounding out a greeting.

'Good afternoon. My name is Thermal. Welcome to our home.'

The old man stroked his head and Thermal walked up his chest to have a closer look at his cap.

'You're a grand lad, aren't you?'

15

'*Thank you. You're very kind.*'

I left them to it and went to make a cup of tea. I had been very touched by the old man's reason for not wanting to go home. Romance comes in surprising packages.

'Would you like a sandwich?'

His gums panicked at the thought and were mightily relieved when he declined the offer.

'Right, I'll be just upstairs if you want anything.'

By the time I came down again he'd mastered the remote controls and was changing channels at a rate of knots. Thermal must have talked him through it. He was still tucked up on the old man's knee and William had perched himself on the arm of the chair. They settled down to watch a rerun of *The Likely Lads* on UK Gold. The old man turned to me.

'Can I ashk you shomething?'

'Of course.'

'I heard a woman'sh voice.'

'My wife.'

He still had his cap on and he adjusted it slightly to give himself a little extra thinking time.

'She won't be coming in here, will she?'

His gums shuddered in embarrassment at the thought and tucked themselves in behind his lips.

'No, don't worry. And if you do happen to bump into her she won't be able to see you. She's registered blind.'

'Oh thank God for that,' he said, easing himself back in his chair. 'That'sh grand ish that.'

When the time came for him to make his way down to the dentist the rain was still battering against the window panes, and so I gave him a lift in the car.

'It'sh very good of you.'

'It's no trouble.'

The garage doors had forgotten they were supposed to go up and over and by the time I had shown them what to do I was soaked to the skin. I should have asked him if I could borrow his cap.

Perhaps not. I doubt if the two of them had been separated since birth. He gave it a short sharp tug as he settled himself in the car and the brim twanged happily and bounced back down again.

'Wouldn't you think,' he said, 'that they'd lend you a shpare shet of teeth, jusht to be going on with? Whenever I had a shervice the garage alwaysh made sure I had a courteshy car.'

The perfect day comes in all shapes and sizes. Seeing the kids, the grandchildren, an unexpected cheque in the post. Aileen's lovely face as her fingers stroked the eternity ring.

Today it had arrived courtesy of a set of false teeth. Courtesy teeth. I could just see the dentist's receptionist looking through her records.

'I'm very sorry but Mrs Raynor hasn't brought them back yet. She should have had them here by four o'clock – it's very naughty of her.'

Perhaps they would carry discreet advertising, like the courtesy car I borrowed from the Body Shop while they were busy putting mine back together again. They had their name written all over the door and it was very effective. A woman came up to me in the multi-storey car park and asked my advice on essential oils.

A letter printed on each tooth. That was it. *False Teeth, courtesy of . . .* – I pulled the car to a halt and glanced at the dentist's nameplate – *Townend, Denham, Millington-Smith and Luty*. No, perhaps not. Bit of a mouthful, that.

They would need something a little more racy. *Supertooth* or *Gnashers Galore*? No, still not quite right.

The old man had one leg out of the door and was about to step out onto the pavement. He half turned and gave me a great big smile.

'Thank you very much,' he said. 'You're very kind.'

It came to me in a flash. *Gums R Us*. That was it. I shall patent the idea and make a fortune.

'No, really,' I replied as he waved goodbye. 'Thank *you*.'

Chapter Two

I gave the cat flap a quick squirt of WD40. That's about as technical as I get. The cat flap is on its last legs and no wonder. It handles more traffic than the turnstiles at Wembley stadium.

There was a time when it stood proudly at the cutting edge of technology, an electronic wonder that opened and shut whenever the cats' collars gave it the password.

Nowadays it just hangs on in there, wincing every time a furry little head bops it in the stomach. Denton started the rot. He's a ginger tom from down the road, built like a brick outhouse and as thick as two short planks. He has spent his entire life at the cutting edge of total ignorance.

And yet it didn't take him long to come up with a solution. He would sit outside, waiting for one of our cats to come bounding out, and then he would catch the cat flap with one paw before it could swing to.

Once in he would mop up enough food for a whole army. His only problem was that he couldn't get out, not until one of the residents came bounding back in again. That's how I caught him. He was waiting by the cellar door with his paw cocked ready, and his overloaded stomach slung close to the ground.

If a thicko like Denton could crack our security system then it wasn't worth a light. Our new-found technology had been downgraded from white hot to stone-cold sober in no time at all. Collars mysteriously went missing and the cat flap swung open to all comers.

We began to welcome a string of no-hopers, an endless procession of beaten-down losers in search of a square meal and a bed for the night.

I had fixed the cat flap in the cellar because I wasn't about to cut holes in solid oak doors that are over a hundred years old. The cellar would serve as a halfway house, I thought, and it couldn't have worked out better.

It's very cosy. The central heating boiler stokes the place up to gas mark 37 and there's a perfectly good carpet that didn't quite match the new three-piece suite. Light pours in through a window set halfway up the cellar steps, illuminating a vast array of extras designed to maximize feline potential. For the musically inclined a piano stands in one corner, and my sturdy old Amstrad sits on the workbench, should they wish to hone their literary skills.

They have an elderly microwave oven which still works in ten-second bursts, long enough for a medium-rare mouse, and there's a television set that is quite capable of receiving BBC2 if the wind is in the right direction and nobody moves.

Best of all there's a vast collection of cat baskets, gathered from some of the finest second-hand shops in West Yorkshire, each of them fitted with a plumped-up cushion to ensure maximum creature comfort.

And yet every morning, when I go down to feed this shifting population, I find them fast asleep on the piano, under the piano, in the sink, up on the top shelf, literally on a bed of nails. Anywhere but in the custom-built accommodation.

Arthur was the first stray to arrive. Tigger found him in the park and brought him home. Both his back legs had been broken and so had his tail, but his dignity was still intact. I always imagined he might have been a town councillor in a previous existence. One of those decent, working-class chaps. Miner's helmet during the day and a bowler hat by night, circa 1928. I remember him from a photograph I once saw hanging on the Town Hall staircase. Never made Mayor, but he could have if he hadn't always put others first.

Two hundred and seventy-one pounds' worth of vet's fees later Arthur decided to repay me by moving in permanently, and he was worth every penny. It broke my heart when he died a couple of years later.

Others come and go. Little Chap appears once a fortnight and I can't make him out. He's the mildest, gentlest, most civilized of cats and yet he chooses to live a life full of drugs, booze and women.

So every two weeks or so we dry him out, feed him up and let him sleep for twenty-four hours. Then he's off out with the lads again. I keep telling him he needs a hobby – he says he's got one.

My WD40 had worked wonders on the cat flap and I was out weeding the garden when Little Chap staggered up the side path and collapsed in a heap in the court-yard.

'Just give me a minute, old son, and I'll be with you.'

He half sat up, wondering how he could stop this paving stone from going round and round. He slid his bum over on to the adjoining slab, but that one was just as bad, and so he decided to lie down, close his eyes and let his mind and body go with it.

'Why on earth do you do it?'

I'm sure he would have answered me if he'd had any idea where the voice was coming from. He half opened one eye, grinned at the stone mushroom and fell fast asleep. I would take him down to the cellar as soon as I had sorted out this weed.

I have never been able to understand why people who come over as all weak and watery are said to be weeds. Those posh plants with their double-barrelled names and a family tree as long as your arm, with roots that go way back, they don't know they're born.

'My dear, I simply can't cope with this soil – far too acid for my liking. And look, there's a horrid little stone in the way. It's just too much.'

Reared under glass and spoilt to death, they are a load of old pansies. Not at all like the weeds who embarrass them by moving in next door. The weeds are tough and wiry. The sort of plant you need on your side when war is declared and the going gets tough.

Especially this little devil. If I had to guess I would say he was one of a large family brought up in Tesco's car park just outside Leeds, where his mother had had to force her way up through two feet of concrete for her first glimpse of daylight. He was determined that his own kids were going to have a better start in life and so when the time came to move on he drifted for miles until he floated over Greenhead Park. Then a crosswind caught him and he missed it by fifty yards or so. Never mind, perhaps it was for the best. The gardeners over there were professionals and would have had him on his bike in no time at all. Whereas over here his opponent was a bit of a prat who couldn't tell one end of a trowel from the other. He had never had it so good and he wasn't giving in easily.

I had been digging him out for months now and he always came back for more. Cut his arms and his legs off and he'd head-butt you.

'Come on – make my day.'

I filled in the hole, raked over the soil and covered it with three inches of forest bark. Down below I could hear the stretcher-bearers going about their duty.

'We can rebuild him.'

Make no mistake – he'd be back.

Little Chap has his favourite spot in the cellar, an old deckchair with a bellying canvas that almost touches the floor. The other cats prefer to be high up on the top shelf, tucked just underneath the ceiling out of harm's way. When I push open the door in the morning they look like a row of targets on a fairground shooting gallery.

But when Little Chap staggers in through the cat flap he needs to collapse somewhere handy. More often than not this will be on the concrete floor, just short of the carpet, and he will lie there, a couple of feet inside the cat flap, until his kindly landlord comes and picks him up and arranges his limbs neatly on the deckchair.

This time he hadn't even made it as far as the door, and so I scooped him up off the paving stone and carried him, limp and bedraggled, down the cellar steps.

I used to worry about him. The first time he arrived I thought he was dying, so I had him up at the vet's before you could say worming powder. They gave him an injection but couldn't find anything wrong with him.

'He's just knackered.'

They told me to feed him up and let him rest, which I did – only the other way around. He slept for the best part of a weekend and then on Monday morning he marched right into the kitchen and played hell with me.

'*Food*.'

He has a way with words. He stretches them. If I don't attend to him immediately he goes straight into overdrive.

'*Foo-oo-oo-ood*.'

It's very effective. But right now all he wanted to do was sleep. The eye that had quivered slightly as I elbowed open the cellar door closed again as I laid him gently in the deckchair. His left ear had turned itself inside out and tucked itself under his cheek. I flicked it and it twanged to attention. That was better. He'd be all right now.

My life is full of contradictions. Most of it is spent at home, with bursts of creativity constantly interrupted by the need to feed and nurture an army of short-haired cats and a long-haired woman.

Aileen plays her part. She deals with the day-to-day accounts and specializes in arranging amazingly good deals and terrifying tradesmen. They can't pull the wool over her eyes. Nature did that years ago and so she never sees the pain on their faces as she asks them if they wouldn't mind doing that again please, and properly this time.

Since she bought me a wok my cooking has come on in leaps and bounds. I can now stir-fry with the best of them, but there are times when it's nice to opt out of the domestic grind and hop onto the celebrity circuit for a change, where someone else does the cooking and I get spoilt to death.

Today I was off to talk at a literary lunch down in the Midlands. I was about to drive out of the car wash when the lady came over to have a word with me. I don't know her name. I know her only as the Lady with the Limp.

She does go on a bit, so I wound down the window and asked if she would mind meeting me over by the pumps so that I could get the car fed and watered while we talked.

I had already taken fifty pounds' worth of unleaded petrol on board by the time she arrived and my mind had slipped inexorably into that boring mode where it insists on reminding me that my mortgage was only eleven pounds, twelve shillings and threepence a month when I first married.

Her limp seems to be getting worse. Since Christmas it appears to have developed a secondary limp all of its own, a somewhat theatrical version of the original, and I felt rather guilty at having dragged her over here.

'Sorry, but I'm in a bit of a hurry.'

She never listens to what you say. I have learned over the years that every Monday morning she comes out of the house with a fresh topic of conversation, honed to perfection over the weekend, and then she tries it out on everyone she meets. Sometimes she has the sense to realize that it's running out of steam by Wednesday and so she'll switch to something else, but more often than not she can keep it going for the full seven days.

It's all rather sad and I'm usually more than happy to give her as much time as she needs, but I was cutting things rather fine today.

'It's my brother.'

Her brother crops up rather a lot. He was once bitten by a dog and she thought he might have rabies. Did I think it was serious? A partridge he shot fell out of the sky and landed on his head and she thought he might have concussion. Did I think it was serious?

'What's happened to him now?'

'He's dead.'

Now that did sound serious. Just about as serious as you can get.

'Oh. I'm very sorry.'

I lifted the bonnet and inserted the dipstick while she told me all about it. Given his past record I did think he might have tried a little harder, put some effort into making his final exit that bit more entertaining. Apparently he died in bed, as a result of being very old.

But just as I thought he'd let me down, his sister came at me with a second wave.

'You know he was a gillie up in Scotland, a sort of gamekeeper?'

I didn't, but it was easier to say yes. It also went some way towards explaining the partridge.

'Well, he says in his will that he wants to be buried on the estate, out on the moors where he worked.'

I thought that was very romantic and I told her so, but she wasn't listening.

'What I want to know is – can they do that? I thought you had to be buried in creosoted ground.'

The thought sustained me all the way through a four-mile tail-back on the M42 and just about made up for me missing the soup, the main course and the summer pudding.

I did manage to grab a cup of coffee, only to find that it had been brewed from a wartime recipe when you couldn't get coffee, which made me feel that perhaps missing the meal hadn't been such a bad thing after all.

A lady leaned over from next door but one on the top table and told me that she was supposed to introduce me.

'Do you write your books under your own name?'

It's surprising how often that one crops up. It meant that she'd never read a single word of mine and hadn't even heard of me before today. I have been tempted more than once to say that no, I write all my books under the pseudonym of Dick Francis.

'No. I call myself Dick Francis.'

Her eyes widened.

'Oh. I've heard of you.'

Before I could stop her she was on her feet, but then so was Madam Chairman who had been sitting between us and heard every word. She took over, with all the authority of a woman who owns a large chain of dress shops and knows exactly what she's doing.

'I'll see to this, Rita.'

She gave me a wonderful and very knowledgeable introduction and then a sharp kick on the ankle as she sat down.

'Forty minutes,' she said. 'No more.'

Thermal was waiting for me on the gatepost when I arrived home. It was way past his teatime. He was weak with hunger and not best pleased.

'That woman trod on me.'

'Well, you know Aileen can't see you. You have to keep out of her way.'

I opened the door and let him in. The others were nowhere to be seen but they wouldn't be long. They can hear a tin being opened at three hundred paces. I filled four saucers with Whiskas duck and turkey in gravy and took one down to the cellar for Little Chap.

They must be using a new recipe these days, I thought. At one time the gravy looked good enough to eat, but now the glaze seemed to disappear very quickly. One minute the bowl of Whiskas looked as though

27

somebody had recently been at it with a varnish brush and the next it was just a pile of uninteresting lumps leaning against each other, bored out of their skulls.

This one seemed right enough, but Little Chap was in no condition to take advantage of it. Curled up on his deckchair like a Danish pastry, he was still out like a light.

I was on my way back up the stairs when the truth dawned on me. I nipped out through the back door and peered in through the kitchen window. Thermal was moving along the line of saucers, his tongue flashing in and out like a little pink spatula on speed. I had caught him red-handed, but he denied it of course.

'*I never.*'

'Oh yes you did. I saw you.'

'*You mean you were spying on me?*'

'I was keeping an eye open.'

He thought that was despicable. If we couldn't trust each other, he said, what future did we have as a family unit?

But I was ready for him.

'And what future do we have if you go licking the gravy off everyone else's Whiskas?'

'*I was testing it.*'

'It doesn't need testing.'

'*Oh, so we're an expert on cat food now, are we?*'

He stormed off in a huff and Thermal in a huff is something to behold. He beat the living daylights out of Aileen's fireside rug and then belted several small ornaments off the mantelpiece, before setting about a poor innocent little toilet roll who had never hurt anyone in his life.

Eventually his huff sent him off across the lane where Bridie would take him in and spoil him and tell him what a clever boy he was. It must have been getting on for midnight before he came back and told me all about it.

Apparently he's worried about all this BSE. His theory is that the answer lies in the gravy. BSE has a bitter taste to it, he says, and he can tell it straight off. His dad once worked with the caretaker at the Technical College, so he knows all about it.

As senior cat he decided it was his task to sample each meal and maybe even lay down his life for the others. Isn't that wonderful? I had tears in my eyes before he had finished. He's an example to us all.

Chapter Three

Before the interview began, she smiled and told me she had read all my books, which is always comforting and not usually the case with radio presenters.

'You seem to like women.'

'I do.'

She glared at the two men who were drinking tea from cardboard cups on the other side of a glass partition. I may have imagined it, but the two of them seemed to be melting slightly at the edges.

'Not like this bloody lot here.'

She pushed her chair away from the console, leaned back and stretched her arms high above her head. Her legs went on for miles and miles before disappearing under a shiny leather pelmet she had slung around her waist. I tried hard not to look at them and failed miserably.

'They think we're only good for one thing,' she growled, nodding her head towards the two men, who had now decided to drink their tea standing up.

'Whereas you look at a woman from the inside, don't you?'

Yes. Any minute now, I thought. If she leans back an

inch further. But then thankfully the red light changed to green and we were on the air.

She was very good at her job and even managed a few questions I had never been asked before, but there is the one that crops up time and time again.

'Do all these things really happen to you?'

'Of course they do.'

'You don't make them up?'

'Of course I don't.'

But I don't think she believed me and I just can't understand why. My adventures are very small adventures that could happen to anyone. Like most people I bumble through as best I can, through a life filled to the brim with the mundane and the microscopic. And yet rarely a day passes without it suddenly deciding to take off at right angles.

As it did on the way home. I got lost. From an island on the ring road I suddenly found myself in the middle of an industrial estate and then in a car park surrounding an out-of-town Asda, before magically entering a motorway service station from the wrong side, down a one-way country lane and in past a sign that read *Lorries Only*.

There were trucks of all shapes and sizes. Some parked up for the night, others manoeuvring and unloading. They towered above me, making me feel like a little lad on a bicycle. I decided to get the hell out of there, the way I came in.

I reversed back up the one-way lane, keeping a mere half an eye on the rear-view mirror as I stared straight ahead through the windscreen, hoping that any casual passer-by would think I was going forward and not backwards.

'Hey, look. His wheels seem to be going the wrong

way round, just like they do in the movies. Isn't that amazing?'

The narrow lane was no more than half a mile long and I had almost made it when a fleet of enormous lorries appeared, shipping in emergency supplies of frozen chips and fun-sized Mars bars. The drivers pipped encouragingly and waved at me with clenched fists as they hauled their pantechnicons out of my way and up onto the grass verge.

I smiled and waved back. We are all part of the same brotherhood, I suppose.

Half an hour later I was hopefully heading north on one of those dual carriageways that have been handcrafted out of solid concrete in order to make you think your tyres have gone flat.

I realized I was going in the wrong direction entirely when I saw the radio station looming up on my left once more, so I pulled off the road and into its car park to try to work out just where I had been going wrong, and to have a quick look at my tyres.

The station had been buttoned up for the night. Just a single light showed in an upstairs window from where an agony aunt was doling out advice to the sad and the lonely. I switched on the car radio.

'. . . and don't forget. If you have a problem just ring me on . . .'

'How the hell do I get out of this place?' I shouted up at the lighted window but she took no notice of me and in no time at all she was up and running once more, dishing out advice to a young man who suffered from terminal acne.

Over on the corner of the road opposite, jutting out into the pavement like a double-breasted battleship, there was either a very popular pub or a penal institution for young offenders – it was hard to tell which. Most of the ground floor windows had been boarded up like a kennel in a Tom and Jerry cartoon, with great rough wooden crosspieces and six-inch nails.

A couple of seriously bald bouncers stood guard at the main entrance, enforcing a strict dress code. If you were a man you had to wear a vest and have had your ears pierced, while the women were required to leave their navels uncovered for inspection at all times.

An unmarked police car with its windows all steamed up was parked right across from the pub, so I decided to go and ask if they could point me towards the A38. It was one of those anonymous white panda cars that creep up behind you when you are doing fifty in a built-up area and there were two men sitting in the front seats. One wore a purple padded anorak with orange sleeves and the other one had more sense.

I tapped on the glass and waited as the electrics buzzed and the window slowly wound its way down. They had a huge thermos flask stuck between them and enough sandwiches to last a lifetime.

'Yes?'

'I'm sorry to bother you, but could you direct me towards the A38?'

They glanced quickly at each other and then the officer in the passenger seat leaned across his col-league's knee to face me.

'How would we know?'

'Well, you're policemen. Aren't you?'

They exchanged glances once more and then the driver casually leaned back in his seat, the tip of his cigarette dancing in time with his lips.

'And what makes you think that?'

'Well, you've got one of those blue lamp things stuck on the roof of the car.'

His eyes snapped shut and the cigarette froze in his mouth.

'Oh shit.'

His hand crept up out of the open window, his fingers exploring the roof until they came across the lamp. He plucked it off its suckers and pulled it inside the car without even looking at it, as though it had never existed, and shoved it down in the well by his feet. Then the window buzzed once more and slowly wound its way up, shutting me out.

I didn't even smile until I was back in my car, conscious that they would be watching me through the rear-view mirror. I wondered how long they had been parked there on plain clothes surveillance – a couple of weeks judging by the quality of the cigarette smoke in the car. I wanted to run into the radio station and tell them.

'You see it does happen, and right outside your own windows.'

It was ages before I came across the A38 and even then I found I was heading down south instead of up north. But what the hell – it had been worth it.

My friend Trevor Evans told me that he was once on plain clothes duty in a shopping mall, as part of a highly trained surveillance team. They were in constant radio contact with one another. He was wearing his Sunday best suit, a crisp white shirt and an Abercrombie overcoat, when a woman rushed up to him.

'Excuse me, officer. I've lost my little girl.'

They searched around and found the child, who had come to no harm, and then Trevor asked the mother how she had managed to crack his disguise.

'Tell me, how did you know I was a policeman?'

The woman, who was in the midst of a joyous re-union, alternately hugging and then belting the living daylights out of her small daughter, paused for a moment and looked up.

'You kept mumbling into your jacket.'

Little Chap was fast asleep when I arrived home, just the other side of the wrought-iron gate so that I couldn't push it open without disturbing him. I bent down and whispered through the bars.

'Come on, now. Let's be having you.'

As usual he seemed to have fashioned himself a cosy little hollow in the middle of a paving stone and was flat on his back with all four legs stuck up in the air. Charming is a word that springs to mind. Gormless is another.

I pushed the gate open very gently at first. I didn't want to alarm him and in that respect I succeeded beyond my wildest dreams. He had no idea he was being swept slowly across the path by a wrought-iron gate until he found himself nestling on a pile of dead leaves that had settled down in the far corner for the duration.

Then a pungent mixture of indignation and rotting foliage brought him bouncing back into the land of the living. He scrambled to his feet and threw back his head.

'*Foo-oo-oo-ood.*'

William watched in deepest admiration from his grand-stand seat on top of the gatepost. He would never dare do that. For all his energy and enthusiasm he still can't quite believe his luck.

After what must have been several months of self-catering out there in the wild, he still can't believe that he has at last hit upon a place where they serve a full English breakfast every morning, a little light lunch around noon and a nourishing evening meal with all the trimmings. Give or take the gravy.

No, it was too good to last and he wouldn't dream of rocking the boat. Most of the time he takes his new life in his stride, picking up tips here and there from the other two residents on what is to be expected of a young cat around the house.

But he still has days when his old insecurities come rushing back to wrap themselves around him like a shroud. Sometimes, if I make a sudden move towards him, he will race from the room and hide until he feels it's safe to come out, or at least until he has forgotten exactly why he happens to be cowering under the single bed in the spare room.

He peered down at the indignant little furball who was still standing four-square by my feet, his head thrown back, demanding to be fed immediately. You never know. It might be worth a try.

'*Foo-oo-oo-ood.*'

'Oh shut up, William.'

'*Sorry. My mistake. Oh my God, I've gone and done it now.*'

I could hear Aileen up in her office tapping away at her computer. She could be working on her new book or taking a little time out to surf the Internet.

I don't delve into the deeper possibilities of the computer. The journey from Amstrad to Compaq laptop in just under twenty years has been quite heady enough for me. There are some things I can't take in. I have to reread the manual every time I use the fax machine. It's nothing to be proud of – quite the opposite – but I have learned over the years that when it comes to modern technology, if I am going to take in something new, then something that I have already stored in my head has to be sacrificed to make room for it. Since I mastered the Compaq I can no longer remember what all the lights and switches are for on the car dashboard and I confuse the stalks on either side of the steering wheel, the one for the windscreen wiper and the other for the horn. It makes for some interesting journeys.

But when it comes to rustling up six individual meals in a matter of a few minutes then I'm your man.

I fed Little Chap first, otherwise he would have started on the hearthrug.

'*Foo-oo-oo-ood.*'

He hadn't eaten for a day and a half to my knowledge and it could have been much longer. I had checked on him before I left home. He was fast asleep. His food had been left untouched and he would have needed a hammer and chisel to fight his way through the thick black crust, so now he nearly tore the saucer out of my hand as I plonked it down in front of him.

The other three cats sat and watched, dumbstruck and awestruck, as he plunged his head deep into the pile of Whiskas tuna and chicken, seeming to take in as much through his ears and nose as he did through his mouth.

As he came up for air Tigger turned away in disgust and then strolled over to the low shelf by the wine rack, where she keeps an open packet of Walkers barbecued beef and onion crisps, jammed in among a set of Japanese tea cups that look very pretty but are far too small to be of any use.

Thermal tagged along behind. He has never been able to manage a whole barbecued beef and onion crisp on his own, they make his eyes water, but he quite likes to mop up the crumbs afterwards.

Tigger reached a paw through the gallery rail and expertly plucked from the packet a large fat crisp, a healthy young male by the look of him, and then she hurled it over her shoulder onto the carpet by the dining table.

She's learned over the years that a cat hasn't been engineered for eating crisps on a smooth kitchen floor. They tend to lie flat, hugging the lino, and her nose gets in the way as she chases them round as she would an ice hockey puck, whereas on the carpet they lodge in the pile, standing tall and proud, just asking for it.

She steadied the crisp between her two front paws and then delicately nibbled all round the outside edge until she had reduced it from a reasonable facsimile of Greenland to an absolutely perfect scale model of the Isle of Man.

Then she turned it upside down and finished it off, starting at the Point of Ayre and working her way up towards Castletown, leaving Thermal to mop up the port of Douglas as far inland as Union Mills and as far north as Onchan while she ambled over to the shelf for seconds.

Little Chap was halfway through his pudding by the time I managed to feed the other three. He'd had Whiskas tuna and chicken for starters followed by a main course of Whiskas tuna and chicken, with a sizeable portion of Whiskas tuna and chicken on the side. For pudding he chose a small tin of Sainsbury's tuna in brine. Apparently it made a nice change.

'Coffee?'

'*No. I couldn't, really.*'

'Chocolate mint?'

'*Perhaps later.*'

Three small heads turned away in unison from their

individual saucers as they watched him waddle off down to the cellar, as fine an example of synchronized gawping as I have seen in a long time. Then two of the heads swivelled back to the business in hand while Thermal turned and glared long and hard in my direction.

'I had to feed him first. It was an emergency.'

Thermal considered this for a moment. And when Thermal considers something he considers it with his whole being. His forehead furrows until you could almost screw his ears off and then the shock wave travels the length of his body, before finally being released into the community with a petulant flick of the tail.

'As long as it doesn't become a habit.'

Aileen and I discussed the welfare of our itinerant lodger over dinner. I had prepared a herb salad with feta cheese and roasted peppers, followed by fiorelli pasta in mushroom and garlic sauce, garnished with squares of bacon, asparagus tips and sweetcorn. I mention this only to point out exactly what can be achieved in ten minutes flat, to prove that my cooking has come on in leaps and bounds over the past few years, and to show off unashamedly.

Aileen is very encouraging. More often than not, when she first comes to the table she hasn't the slightest idea what is on the menu, and she still can't see what I have set down before her once she has taken her seat, with her head hovering just inches above her plate. But she is always ready with an enthusiastic word or two.

'Oh, lovely. I smell tuna.'

For some time now I had been worrying about Little Chap and wondering whether or not to have him neutered. But he never seemed to stay conscious long enough for me to take him to the vet. When he wasn't sleeping he was eating and when he wasn't either eating or sleeping, he wasn't here.

Apart from that he wasn't really my cat. He didn't seem to have a home of his own, but he was most certainly house-trained. He never sprayed, always popped out to use the toilet and then made sure to leave it as he would have expected to find it.

Most of the time he stayed down in the cellar, where Tigger had taken him the first time she brought him home, half starved and as weak as a kitten. He was much smaller than Thermal then and scared to death of him until he realized that Thermal was nothing more than a big soft kid at heart, and now he occasionally came up into the house and mingled with the others for a moment or two.

This would usually be on the day before he left for yet another walk on the wild side. He would stick close to Tigger as she took him on a tour of the establishment and he would make a half-hearted attempt to show interest in her new padded scratching post, complimenting her on her good taste.

But you could see he was becoming rather edgy and it wouldn't be long before he made his excuses and took to the courtyard, where he would pace the perimeter wall for a good hour or so before suddenly leaping down the other side and racing off towards the park and another two or three weeks of dissipation.

He would make a break for it tomorrow by my reckoning, after a good night's sleep and a nourishing breakfast of Whiskas tuna and chicken on toast.

Aileen chased a rogue asparagus tip round and round her plate. It wasn't the sort to give up easily, so eventually she abandoned her fork and went after it with forefinger and thumb. With nowhere to hide it cowered as far away as possible, holding its breath until the inevitable happened. I felt sorry for it.

'That was very nice.'

'Thank you.'

I poured freshly ground coffee from the cafetière and then spent some time with a teaspoon, removing a flotilla of little bits and pieces from each cup. I've become used to the little devils now. I take my time about it and wait for the stragglers to come up for air.

'Do you think I should take Little Chap to be seen to?'

'He's heading for an early grave otherwise.'

It did seem to be the obvious thing to do and yet I had my doubts. He was a free spirit. He could have settled down with us, but instead he had chosen a life of wine, women and song. We don't do a lot of singing in our house.

'It's like taking Oliver Reed to be neutered.'

'In that case I'm all for it.'

The next morning, armed with a rather swish cat transporter and accompanied by Thermal as my personal cat translator, I went down to the cellar to get him.

'Be sure to tell him it doesn't hurt.'

'*You tell him. I was sore for a week.*'

Little Chap was fast asleep on the boiler as I pushed open the door, but after a healthy yawn and a really good stretch he made us most welcome. In fact he made it all too easy for me.

He jumped down and strolled over to the pet carrier, sniffed appreciatively at the plastic door hinges and then walked inside.

'*Rather well made, isn't it?*'

I closed the door behind him and carried him out of the cellar. Thermal followed us upstairs.

'You wouldn't have got me as easily as that.'

Cats have a way of making you feel guilty. If Little Chap had lost his temper I could have coped with that, but he just sat imprisoned on the passenger seat of the car, staring at me through the bars with his big blue eyes.

'I never thought you would stoop to such a trick.'

I felt even worse on the way back. Little Chap had decided he wanted no part of this, so the vet had had to coax him out by standing the carrier on its end and tipping him onto the table. It must be hell being smaller than everyone else. The vet had given him a cursory examination and then handed him over to me.

'He's already been done.'

Thermal was taunting a small Yorkshire terrier when we arrived home, but as soon as he saw the car pull into the side road he jumped down from the wall and led us into the courtyard.

'It was a much longer job in my day.'

As soon as I pulled back the bolts of his cage Little Chap was off and I can't say I blame him. He made straight for the wrought-iron gate and squeezed between the bars. He didn't even look back and by the time Thermal and I reached the end of the path he had already negotiated the narrow road and was streaking off across the park.

A large Alsatian gave chase but was soon pulled up short by his extending lead, and an old mongrel who wouldn't have been seen dead on a lead – not in a million years – thought about it for a moment or so and then decided to carry on watering his tree.

Thermal and I walked back up the path together. The carrier sat all forlorn in the courtyard with the door standing wide open. I picked it up and took it down the cellar steps. Thermal raced on ahead of me.

'Got any more bright ideas?'

Chapter Four

There is something wonderful about being married to a woman who will wait for me on the wrong street corner, casually chatting up an alarming young man who is being given a wide berth by everyone else in the vicinity. She couldn't see him of course, but she thought he was charming.

'He had a lovely big dog with him. It licked my hand.'

It was a Rottweiler.

'He said he was from Manchester.'

I guessed as much. He had *Man Utd* tattooed lengthways up both arms, along with *Mum* and *Dad* on either side of his neck, and the individual letters of *Love* and *Hate* were stamped upon each of his fingers. A red and blue snake reached up from underneath his T-shirt and was about to make a meal of his Adam's apple before going on to have a swing on the ring through his left nostril.

He hung on for a while after I arrived but then, tossing the remains of his burger and French fries down on the pavement, he turned and lurched off in the general direction of Market Square.

'He wanted to know where the church was.'

I watched him cross the road and carry on down towards the parish church. He had a small haversack slung over one shoulder. He wouldn't get much lead in that. Perhaps the Rottweiler had a van parked nearby, ready for a quick getaway.

'Come on. I'll buy you lunch at the Theatre Bar.'

We always seem to have so much to talk about. I find that amazing. Two people who spend each and every day together, working, eating and sleeping, ought to have nothing left to say and yet we never shut up. Except when we take time out and indulge in a little eavesdripping, as Aileen puts it.

Our conversation gradually ground to a halt as we tuned in to the two women nattering away at the next table. One of them had moved with the times – almost, and was power-dressed from top to toe in chain-store Versace, with huge pads that sat to attention on each of her shoulders, like two stone lions either side of the steps of a municipal building.

Her companion had decided to stay put in the 1950s and it suited her. She wore a shapeless cloth coat, belted around her considerable middle, and had topped off the ensemble with a matching felt hat. The fact that it matched the curtains behind her rather than the coat she wore only added to the charm of the outfit.

They were deep in conversation, verbally disembowelling a mutual acquaintance.

'He's a bad 'un, is that one, Jessie,' muttered Shoulder Pads, her earrings swinging indignantly as she tossed her head. 'I wouldn't give him the time of day.'

'Oh come on now, Beryl. There's some good in everyone.'

'Not in him there isn't.'

'Yes, there is, love. As long as you're prepared to look for it.'

There was a pause as Beryl, as we had now come to know her, racked her brains for the killer punch.

'Oh aye. What about Adolf Hitler then?'

There was an even longer pause as Jessie considered this and then, folding her arms across her chest, she finally admitted defeat.

'Well yes, I must admit I could never quite *warm* to him.'

All the way home Aileen carried on the conversation, leaning back in her seat with her bare feet stuck up on the dashboard – an exercise which completely defeats the object of her wearing a seat belt in the first place and means that in the event of an accident her knees will be driven straight through her ribcage. I've told her a thousand times, but still she takes no notice.

'Anthony Hopkins in *Silence of the Lambs*. Now I could never quite warm to him.'

'Put your feet down.'

'Joseph Stalin – I could never quite warm to him either.'

'If we have an accident you'll finish up about three foot tall.'

'Mickey Mouse. Now he's another one I never could quite warm to.'

'If I have to brake sharply you'll – Mickey Mouse?'

'Little tosspot, with that high squeaky voice of his. Absolutely no talent whatsoever. Never could stand him. Not a patch on Tom and Jerry.'

I drove home in silence, listening to her as she vented her wrath on Colonel Gaddafi, Idi Amin and Francis the talking mule. So much to learn about her – so little time.

* * *

She wasn't warming to Gerry Adams as we walked up the garden path. A young woman had seen us coming and was waiting patiently on the front step. She had with her a little girl, the type of kid you don't often see around these days – washed, ironed and pre-shrunk and wearing a dress straight out of *Little House on the Prairie*.

They smiled identical smiles – the sort of smile that forgives you, for you know not what you do. These smiles have a mission to explain. To them, every day is a Sunday and they are determined that you should listen to their half-baked ideas. This was the sort of smile that should have been strangled at birth.

'Do you love animals?'

I mean, what sort of a question is that? She had a regular army of cats milling around her feet, waiting for me to stick the key in the front door, and young William had gone and perched himself on her left foot, looking for all the world like a very small vicar with his shiny black coat and gleaming white ruff. He smiled at me. The sort of smile that says it is suffering from acid indigestion and is about to break wind at any moment.

Aileen had stopped short at the sound of the voice.

'Who is it?'

'It's a young lady – two young ladies. I think they have come to tell us about God.'

'*He* loves animals,' declared the young woman as I pushed open the door.

'I should hope he does,' muttered Aileen. 'What sort of God would he be if he didn't love animals?'

The two of them smiled at her, oozing tolerance from every pore. Good job she couldn't see them.

I rather enjoy a good religious debate. I always lose in the end. Should I find myself ahead at any particular

stage then I get terribly embarrassed about it and con-
cede the point immediately. Besides, letting the other
person win always makes them feel better and isn't that
what Christianity is all about? Of course, it is also what
cowardice is all about.

Aileen on the other hand, with her clear, crisp mind,
employs a lethal brand of cold, hard logic to destroy the
opposition and where's the fun in that?

The older of the two girls had just launched herself
into a well-rehearsed sales pitch when I glanced down
the path and noticed something missing.

'Oh, my God!'

I don't think she had ever made such an instant
conversion in her short life and it took her completely
by surprise. She paused and took a deep breath, ready
to press home her advantage.

'My balls have gone.'

The girl reached out an arm and drew her young
companion close to her side. The Lord might have
rendered me harmless but she was taking no chances. I
turned to Aileen, who was busy apologizing to Thermal
for having cracked him around the back of the neck
with her handbag. I pointed down the path.

'They were there when we went out. I'm sure they
were.'

In fact I knew they were. Thermal had waved us off,
his four paws tucked up tightly together as he balanced
precariously, like a performing seal, on one of the two
stone balls that sat on a solid plinth and topped off the
huge stone gateposts.

And now they had gone. The two gateposts stood
bareheaded either side of the wrought-iron gate and I
felt the anger rise in me. They had been up there for
over a hundred years, cemented in and skewered by an
iron rod. It would have taken at least two men to prise

48

them off. Maybe the same two men who turned up with a flat-bed lorry a year ago and carted off my pavement.

I despise thieves. When they are caught I think their favourite possessions should be taken from them and destroyed as a matter of course. An eye for an eye – a ghetto blaster and a twenty-nine-inch television set for two stone balls. Makes sense to me.

Then I remembered the stone mushroom. My grand-mother's, my mother's and now mine, it stood alone in the front garden – serving as a lookout post for all four cats and as a stage for a tap-dancing squirrel who visited every now and then and put on shows for the troops.

I inherited the mushroom along with two stone pig troughs which were now overflowing with soil and flowers and would have needed a JCB to shift them. But the mushroom would be easier meat and it was a great relief to see it was still there.

An unpleasant coating of gunge-covered shell showed that our resident thrush had once again been using it as a chopping board in order to disembowel some poor unfortunate snail, but at least it was untouched by human hand and I could live with the beak. I would have a word with him later and ask if he wouldn't mind tidying up after himself.

Patrick, my neighbour, peered over the hedge. You have to be as tall as Patrick to peer over the hedge. I peered through the branches, at a spot just to the right of his left nipple, as his rich Irish voice brushed against the topmost leaves.

'Have you seen what they've done?'
'Yes.'
'Gone and pinched your balls.'
'I know. I've just found out.'
'Bastards. They want castrating.'

Now there was a thought. An eye for an eye and a ball for a ball. Even more appropriate than the ghetto blaster.

Patrick worries about me. He thinks I am too trusting. He has to restrain himself from frisking the guide-dogs-for-the-blind lady as she's pushing an envelope through his letter box.

'You need to keep a better eye on things.'

'I know.'

'You can't afford to relax for a moment.'

Patrick wandered off to tell his wife Sarah all about it and I thought I had better go in and ring the police. The two girls had made their escape and were now across the road, leaning heavily on Gwen's doorbell. I wished them luck. The doorbell works well enough, but Gwen's hearing doesn't. I always take my mobile phone with me and ring her from her own doorstep. Even so it can take a good half hour – you have to catch her as she's dusting the phone.

The police were much quicker and very sympathetic. There was a lot of it about apparently and did I need counselling? I said I didn't. They had offered us counselling once before, after one of our hanging baskets went missing, but we'd managed to struggle on without it and three years later we had almost come to terms with our loss. Curiously enough, I don't remember anyone asking me if I needed counselling after I found my first wife drowned in the bath.

That afternoon I worked on the screenplay of *Lost for Words*. Yorkshire Television had decided to take a chance on me. They had sunk a lot of money into the project and sets were being built and a cast was being assembled. I was now working on the third draft and hoping that there would be no need for a fourth.

Thermal worked with me. He had already sorted out his paper clips for the day and was now busily chewing the rubber bit off the end of a pencil, quietly, so that he wouldn't interrupt my train of thought. He's very good that way.

Even so my mind kept skipping back to the two stone balls. The thought that somebody must have been casing the joint for some time and then maybe even watched us as we left the house, was unsettling. A phone call to Architectural Antiques of Elland had told us that they would be worth around four hundred and fifty pounds and almost impossible to replace. But it wasn't the money. We had been invaded. Our privacy had been violated and it puts you on edge.

Every now and then I felt the need to leave my desk and go over to the window to see if the garage was still where I had left it. It was, but I had an uneasy feeling that somebody might be round the back, out of sight, slipping castors underneath, ready to roll it away as soon as dusk fell.

Viewed from up above, the gateposts looked like a couple of lonely skinheads waiting at a bus stop, until William decided to do something about it.

He clambered up to the top and then spread himself out in the sunshine, his thick little body immediately upholstering the jarring white of the naked cement, his luxuriant black tail hanging down the side so that his gatepost was turned into a dead ringer for Davy Crockett. Now if I could find myself another cat just like William I might be able to save myself a bob or two . . .

A movement in the front garden caught my eye. Just a flutter under the flowering privet. The thrush perhaps, back with a slug to stir-fry or yet another snail to fricassee. Then I saw the squirrel. A born athlete, he was limbering up with a series of stretching exercises.

51

He is a very professional little squirrel and takes his business most seriously – he believes a pulled muscle to be the mark of an amateur and something to be avoided at all costs.

Thermal had to see this. I plucked him from the desk, hoisted him up on my shoulder and pointed him in the general direction of the front garden. The squirrel had just done a handstand on the garden wall and was about to attempt a triple somersault with half twist and rupture.

'Can you see him? Over on the wall, by the gate.'

Thermal shifted himself slightly and then peered deep into my left ear.

'*I think you've got a bit of wax.*'

'Never mind that.'

I plucked him off my shoulder and held him out to dry in front of me.

'There. Straight ahead of you.'

The squirrel was now performing excerpts from *Riverdance* on a low-lying branch, just to the left of the ornamental chimney pot. He was a natural, but Thermal missed him. He was busily examining a small imperfection in the window sill.

'*You want to touch that up. It'll spread like wildfire.*'

'Never mind that.'

I pressed his body up against the window pane and his nose went a funny shape and spread all over the glass.

'*I can't breathe.*'

'Sorry. I just wanted you to see this. There, look. He's on the stone mushroom.'

The squirrel had chosen the mushroom as the perfect place to take a standing ovation. He bowed to all four corners of the garden and then, somewhat disappointed that no one had thought to throw flowers, he turned and made his way back to the park.

Thermal in the meantime had screwed his head up-side down and was having a good look at the underside of the pelmet.

'You missed it.'

'*Missed what?*'

You can't point a cat at anything. They just don't want to know. They think you are trying it on. Thermal's neck takes on all the qualities of a bendy toy if I so much as attempt to draw his attention to anything in-teresting and his eyes cross over each other until they almost meet up round the back of his neck.

It's so disappointing. I can't really enjoy anything thoroughly unless I share the moment with someone else. If there's a good film on the television and I am on my own, I want to run out and drag people in off the street.

'Here, come and look at this. You'll love it.'

The other cats are just as bad. Tigger comes running to fetch me the instant she spots anything that takes her fancy, such as a spider on the hearthrug.

'*Come and watch this. I'm going to duff him up and I want a witness in case he sues.*'

But if I try to share one of my quality moments with any of them – forget it. The trouble is I can't forget it. I'm a born sharer, and so when the thrush appeared as the next turn on the bill I grabbed hold of Thermal once more.

'Look at that. No, not there – over there by the roses. Can you see him? He's got a huge worm. Yes, I know they're very pretty curtains, but that's not what I'm on about. Look at the thrush, for God's sake.'

I'd have been better off with a glove puppet. I planted Thermal down on the table and watched on my own as the thrush completed his act by tossing the poor worm high in the air before catching it on the way down and swallowing a good two thirds of it. The remaining third wriggled desperately in the vice-like beak for a moment or two, trying to make a break for it. But it wasn't best equipped for such an intricate manoeuvre and finally went the way of all flesh.

Patrick reappeared in his front garden, a spade in one hand and a can of lager in the other. He snapped open the can, rammed the spade deep into the soft earth and sat on the handle. He's my kind of gardener, is Patrick.

Over his head I could see his stone gateposts, exact replicas of mine. Both his balls were missing. Better go and tell him. He'd want to know. A trouble shared is a trouble halved.

Chapter Five

I sat waiting my turn. Four of us were due to speak and I was to be on last. A quarter of an hour each, we had been told, and the young man who was to start the ball rolling was now into his twenty-fifth minute and had just begun to read a great slab from his newly published novel.

At first they were known as the Angry Young Men, and then came the Brat Pack. Nowadays the breed has been watered down by the Martin Amises and Will Selfs of this world and comes under the general heading of the Aren't I a Little Rascal school of literature. This one had spent the first twenty minutes venting his wrath upon London's publishing establishment and it hadn't gone down too well up here in North Yorkshire.

The chairman was the editor of the local newspaper and he'd just about had enough. He rose to his feet. A small man, he had somehow seemed much taller sitting down, but his voice had been honed on junior reporters for more years than it cared to remember and it could take the skin off at forty yards.

'Going to have to stop you there, young man. Sorry to tear you away from yourself, but it's nearly twenty-five to three now and if we go on at this rate we'll none of us be home for *Coronation Street* – and we can't have that, can we?'

The young man sat down, blithely unaware of what a prat he had made of himself, and the chairman introduced the next speaker. She was young and pretty and nervous as hell. The audience took to her immediately and decided to help her along by listening intently and laughing out loud at her occasional jokes.

The young man turned and whispered to the chairman.

'I think I was aiming a bit above their heads.'

'No, not at all, young man. They knew exactly what you were on about – it's just that they didn't give a bugger.'

As I drove home I thought about my very first literary luncheon. There were three of us writers on the bill. The other two had been at the same university, and together they combined to shut me out and make me feel as though I had been brought along to serve the drinks.

One had recently edited a book of historical quotations and the other, a knight of the realm, had spent the latter part of his life as a political commentator for the BBC. He had written about his life and so had I. He recounted personal conversations with Winston Churchill and Clement Attlee and I told the audience about my mother and Nellie Elliot.

I learned something that day. If he's not presented with a certain energy and warmth, Winston Churchill doesn't sell anywhere near as many books as Nellie Elliot, and I was still signing hardback copies long after the other two had given up and gone off to drown their sorrows at the bar.

*　*　*

Since that day I have strutted my stuff at hundreds of these lunches and Aileen says it's because I like to show off. For herself she picks and chooses, because for days before the event her nerves gnaw away at her stomach lining until she's pretty much of a wreck. It's just not worth it. She shakes all the way there. She can't use notes and she can't see the audience, but once she stands up to talk she is quite brilliant and enjoys herself immensely. She can't think why she doesn't do this more often – until the next time.

I enjoy meeting other writers. Some can be a pain in the neck, but on the whole they are a very democratic bunch of people who spend most of their days working in isolation and relish being let out to play. Most of them don't give a toss whether you sailed through university or were thrown out of school at the age of fourteen, whether you write romantic fiction or are rumoured to be heading straight for the Booker Prize. As long as you have started a book and stuck with it for some three hundred pages, then they know the agonies you must have been through and are more than happy to welcome you to the fold.

I also enjoy meeting the readers. It is very rare to come across someone actually reading one of your books. Writing is a solitary business and so, to a certain extent, is reading.

And perhaps it's for the best. Leslie Thomas, of *Virgin Soldiers* fame, once walked into the foyer of a hotel and saw a woman curled up on a settee, engrossed in one of his paperbacks.

'She's reading my book. I'm going to tell her.'

He walked over and sat down beside her.

'Sorry to bother you, but that's my book.'

57

The woman stood up, closed the paperback and handed it over to him.

'Here, you can have it. It was lying on the settee when I came in.'

It's a humbling experience. I was shopping in Marks and Spencer's food hall not so long ago, taking a few minutes out to help one of the staff. She wanted to know where the hell the bags of ready-sliced runner beans had gone and hidden themselves, and since I spend more time in the shop than most of the staff, she naturally asked for my assistance.

I took her over and pointed them out. Marks and Spencer's like to keep their shelves in a continual state of evolution – they don't want us resting on our laurels. No sooner have the unsliced loaves and currant tea-cakes made a comfortable home for themselves on the second shelf down and congratulated one another on finding such a pleasant place to bring up their little baps . . .

'Our family has lived on this very spot for generations, your father and his father before him.'

'How long is that, mam?'

'The Wednesday before last.'

'Wow!'

. . . No sooner have they settled down to a nice quiet life, with an unrestricted view of the wines, spirits and sparkling elderflower cordial, than it's time for the Easter eggs to take centre stage and the poor old loaves find themselves turfed out without so much as a by-your-leave and shoved in a corner next to the tinned cat food and sundry items.

Even I get confused at times, and I was in the process of tracking down a jar of beetroot slices – I prefer the crinkle-cut variety – when I became aware of a navel winking at me from across the aisle.

It was situated halfway between a pair of faded denim jeans and a cotton T-shirt. The T-shirt had been knotted a couple of times in order to allow the navel plenty of room to breathe and it was taking full advantage of its freedom.

'Excuse me.'

I couldn't remember ever having heard a navel talk before, but then I realized that the voice was coming from higher up, from the owner of the navel, a vivacious young woman with a sing-song voice that sparkled just as brightly as her long blond hair and soft golden tan.

'I hope you don't mind . . .'

To hell with the crinkle-cut beetroot. There were more important things in life.

'. . . but my mother would like a word with you, if it's no trouble.'

I hadn't noticed her mother. She was the sort of mother you don't notice. Dressed from head to toe in navy blue – shoes, tights and pleated skirt, with a snow-white Peter Pan collar peeping out from under a navy crew-neck sweater. She moved in on me.

'Sorry to be a nuisance, but are you him?'

I wasn't too sure whether I was him or not.

'Which him would that be exactly?'

'The writer.'

I preened a little, but not so you would notice.

'Yes – that's right.'

She moved in even closer, surrounding me in a sea of navy blue.

'Tell me. What's your name?'

'Deric Longden.'

She thought about it for a moment and then shook her head.

'No,' she said. 'That's not it.' She patted my arm gently. 'Never mind, love – it'll come to me.'

And with that the two of them wandered away, pausing only to pluck a jar of crinkle-cut beetroot from a nearby shelf. I wandered over and picked up a jar myself, but all the fun had gone out of it by then.

Aileen was weeding under the bedroom window as I pushed open the gate and walked up the path. At least *she* knows who I am. She shielded her eyes with a delicate hand and peered in my general direction.

'Who is it?'

'It's me, love.'

She smiled and reached that delicate hand of hers out towards a towering lily with a posh name. It's been in our family for over eighteen months now and is settling in very well. Aileen gave it a tentative yank.

'*No. It's me.*'

'Sorry.'

She felt her way along until she came across a small buttercup who was fooling around with a friend and not paying enough attention. Before he knew what had hit him, he found himself stuffed upside down in a black plastic bucket.

'*Oh sod it.*'

Aileen rose to her feet and gave me a kiss.

'How did the luncheon go?'

I find it very comforting to be married to someone who understands, from personal experience, that some you win and some you lose. One day you might just scrape through by the skin of your teeth and the next day you are quite brilliant. It's the way it is and I can always tell her the honest truth without loss of face.

'I was brilliant.'

'Told you not to worry.'

I was about to tell her just how brilliant I had been when William came racing in through the gate like an electrified spaniel. He was soaked to the skin and we hadn't had a drop of rain for a week.

William is very good at getting soaked. It's what he does best. Three or four times a week he streaks in through the kitchen door, dripping all over the place. At first I wondered if perhaps he was a special breed of cat who just happened to sweat a lot, but now I think that somewhere close by there lives someone who harbours a grudge against him and who keeps a hosepipe cocked and at the ready for whenever William decides to put in an appearance.

I took him into the kitchen and gave him a quick rub-down with a warm towel. He loves that, especially the bit where he lies on his back and I give his tummy a good seeing to, finishing him off by firmly ringing out his tail through both of my hands.

'Any messages?'

'*You were a bit rough with my tail that time. In future, if you could just—*'

'I was talking to Aileen.'

'*Oh. Sorry.*'

Aileen fished her tape recorder from out of her jeans pocket and plonked it down on the kitchen table. It saves her the laborious business of having to make notes, half on little bits of paper and half on the table-cloth. She pressed the play button and we both sat and stared at the little black box as it relayed an edited version of the day's events.

'*Margaret rang. She won't be coming up this week, but she says she'll see you in Leeds next Thursday.*'

Margaret Mathieson is a mover and a shaker. A wonderful lady, she gets things done. She was the executive producer of *Wide-Eyed and Legless* and after coming to see us had taken away the half-finished screenplay of *Lost for Words*. She rang me from London the very next day.

'Finish it.'

Then when the BBC eventually turned it down she told me not to worry. 'I'll get it made if it takes me fifteen years.'

I suggested that perhaps she might put that a little differently when next she spoke to Dame Thora Hird. It's hardly the sort of thing an actress wants to hear when she's fast approaching her eighty-eighth year.

Now Margaret had found a loving home for the play with Yorkshire Television and things were buzzing. Aileen pressed the button once more.

'*Andrew Sanderson would like the large photo of you in your white angora bonnet and your white bootees. Also the one of your mother in Blackpool.*'

Andrew was designing the sets for the play and I was to take pride of place on the mantelpiece in my mother's lounge. Ah, the glory of it all.

The machine cleared its throat once more.

'*And the cats need a bag of fresh litter for their trays and don't forget the bottle bank.*'

Aileen knows how to bring me down to earth, and William illustrated her point by practising one of his famous handbrake turns in his litter tray. Little lumps of damp gravel flew halfway across the kitchen floor and I went off to get the vacuum cleaner before fetching young William a smart clip across the backside.

It's a ten-minute journey up to the bottle bank and back and it usually takes me an hour or so. Something always happens and if it doesn't I hang around until it does.

Those of us who love the village of Marsh know that it lives and breathes and hums with activity, but to the casual motorist, driving up from the centre of Hudders-field towards the M62, it's just another dreary stretch of main road, to be negotiated at sixty miles an hour if at all possible.

They wouldn't notice that Lloyds Bank is about to have a new sign fitted and that while the workmen have nipped off to enjoy a tea break someone has gone and sorted out the pile of old letters and rearranged them under the window so that they now read DONKY BALLS.

At sixty miles an hour they wouldn't see that the old man waiting on the pavement edge has a racing pigeon peeping out of his raincoat pocket. As I pull up to let the two of them cross the road the pigeon looks right and left and then right again before giving me a grateful nod as the old man sets off slowly for the other side.

The casual passer-by wouldn't know how pleased we were when we heard the news that the old carpet shop, which had been boarded up for years, was about to be given a facelift. The Co-op have sold it. It's now a liquor store, all dressed up in black and red and called Booze Busters and at night we sit and think fondly of the good old days when it was tastefully boarded up.

The Co-op have also changed the name of their supermarket further up the road. At first it was Leo's, but now they have stuck in a row of new tills and renamed it the Pioneer. Down in town their large department store has changed its name to Living. I don't know why they bother. People still say, 'If you're going anywhere near the Co-op, get me a bag of sugar and a pound of leeks.'

Still, bless them, they do have a bottle bank round the back of the store. It must be a nightmare for those living in glass-smashing proximity to the bins, but is a boon for us red wine drinkers who live well out of the way and come up with the empties only once a month.

As I nosed my car into the park I happily gave way to a man with a pushcart. He smiled and eased his contraption into a vacant parking space. I hadn't seen anything like it for years. Right out of *Steptoe and Son*, it had been built around four huge pram wheels, dating from the days when prams were a status symbol and roughly the size of the Royal Coach. The wheels had been grafted on to what looked like a wardrobe that had died on its back after a long illness, and two wooden shafts provided the power steering.

I pulled into the space next to him and watched him out of the corner of my eye. He was a short man but he was wearing a pair of very tall trousers that had been especially designed to keep his nipples warm in winter. He wore a coat of many colours – a splash of emulsion here, a dab of gloss there – and a blue and white bobble hat that would have gone well with a fishing rod by the side of a garden pond.

I pushed open the car door and he peered down the length of his cart to make sure I didn't scratch it.

'Nice car.'

'Thank you.'

'What sort is it?'

'It's a Jaguar. A Sovereign.'

'Very nice.'

It is at this point that I always start apologizing for my good fortune.

'It's getting on a bit now. Had it since it was a pup.'

I wanted to tell him how much I admired his pushcart but worried that it might sound patronizing.

He put his nose to the car window and stared in at the seats.

'Leather?'

'Yes.'

'Very nice.'

I desperately wanted to reciprocate.

'Lovely shafts. I bet it can't half shift.'

I moved round to the rear end and flicked open the boot. He followed me and stood by my side. He shook his head sadly.

'Wouldn't do for me. Hardly get owt in there.'

Then his mobile phone went off. He had to dig deep to find it. It was buried in his left-hand trouser pocket, just under his armpit, and he almost dislocated his shoulder in his attempt to locate it. In the end he fished it out through a hole in the lining.

'Hate these things. It'll be my partner.'

It was his partner and he told him that he would meet him in Rochdale later on that evening. I glanced at his pushcart and imagined it belting down the fast lane of the M62.

'Just a minute – got a call waiting.'

He pressed whatever it was he had to press as he wandered away towards the store. It was his wife who was interrupting, apparently, and he was not amused. He didn't like being disturbed during business hours.

I can remember when rag-and-bone men carried balloons about their person. Now it's a mobile phone with Call Waiting and they have fellow directors in Rochdale and they wouldn't even give my Jaguar house room. Once again I had managed to come third in a two-horse race.

Then another contender came up fast on the outside. This time it was a proper tramp – not one of your upwardly-mobile rag-and-bone men. He had all his worldly possessions stuffed in an old supermarket trolley that seemed intent on going sideways, and he stopped by the turbo-charged pushcart and sighed

deeply. One day, if he ploughed all his profits back . . .
He shook his head sadly. No, it was too late for that
now.

He came over to see what I was doing. His trolley had
a mind of its own. It had seen all the other trolleys lined
up behind the Co-op and the herding instinct was still
strong. The tramp wrestled with it until it gave in quietly
and then they both came and stood by my side and
stared at the array of empty bottles in my boot.

'You've been busy.'

'How do you mean?'

'That stuff. You don't half knock it back, don't you?'

'No, I wouldn't say that.'

'I would.'

He shuffled forward a couple of paces and stuck his
head deep in the boot, his lips moving in time with
his brain as he deliberately counted the bottles. It
seemed to take for ever.

'Forty-seven. Forty-seven bottles.'

He straightened and caught sight of the two whisky
bottles I was trying to hide behind my back.

'Forty-nine.'

'Yes. Well, I don't come up here all that often. I stack
them in the cellar until it's worth the trip.'

'Oh aye?'

'Yes. And there are two of us and we have lots of
friends round.'

I couldn't believe I was defending myself like this,
especially to a man who had half a bottle of gin and
a cheese sandwich nestling on that wire tray where
harassed mothers normally plant their toddlers.

'Anyway. Red wine is good for you. Prevents you
having heart attacks.'

He sniffed.

'So that's what they're saying now, is it?'

I reached in and picked up a crate of empties.

'Here, let me give you a hand.'

He took it from me and balanced it on the top of his trolley. The trolley groaned, it was getting too old for this sort of thing, but the tramp somehow found space for the other two as well and the three of us trooped over towards the bins.

I began hurling my collection through the hole in the green bin and my new-found friend grabbed hold of another crate and began to toss the contents into the mouth of the white one.

'They don't go in there.'

'How do you mean?'

'They're green bottles.'

'I know they are.'

'So they go in the green bin.'

He took a pace backwards so that he could get a wider view of the situation.

'You mean they've got a different bin for each colour?'

'Yes.'

'Brown, white and green.'

'Yes.'

'So the brown bottles go in the brown bin and the green bottles go in the . . .'

'That's right.'

He selected four brown bottles and walked over to the brown bin, lobbing them one by one through the hole. Then he turned back the blanket covering his trolley and took out two empty gin bottles that were tucked up among his winter clothing. He dropped them in the white bin with a certain tinge of regret.

'Somebody thought this system up, you know. Sat in an office and thought it up.'

'I suppose they must have done.'

He sighed as we turned back towards the car.

'There's some clever minds about, you know.'

I offered him a couple of pounds for his trouble and he said, no, really I shouldn't, there was no need to, that wasn't why he had given me a hand, if we couldn't help one another without money coming into it then what was the world coming to, and then he took it.

His trolley was still champing at the bit, dying to go and have a word with the free-range trolleys who were hanging out round the back of the Co-op. Some of them were grazing idly in and around the parked cars while a more motivated bunch were all lined up by the ramp, eager to be back on the shop floor. A rather furtive-looking couple of wire baskets seemed to be having sex in the disabled parking bay.

I headed my car out towards the exit and then sat there, waiting for a break in the traffic. Meanwhile the tramp had staggered up the slope with his belongings and begun to road test some of the newer-looking trolleys.

The first one had a fit of the staggers, I could see that from down the other end of the car park. It wobbled from side to side as he tried to keep it in a straight line. The next one seemed a much better bet as he gave it a whirl up and down the ramp before sticking it alongside a Volvo, where he could keep an eye on it while he made his mind up.

All this time the old trolley, jam packed with all his bits and pieces, watched his performance with a nervous eye. Was this the parting of the ways? Was he about to be thrown on the scrapheap? Had it really come to this?

His owner disappeared between two parked cars and came out pushing a bright young thing, all shiny metal and bouncing wheels, that pranced ahead of him like a young colt.

Without a second thought the tramp began to decant his belongings from his faithful old friend, piling them high in the young pretender. And then they were off across the car park without a backward glance. The worn old trolley stood there desolate and abandoned.

I found a gap in the traffic and pulled out into the road. As I curved round the car park I saw the trolley beginning to move. Now the weight had been taken from its shoulders it very slowly began to run backwards down the slope, then, gaining speed, it swung round, dancing across the tarmac like a pit pony released into the sunlight after years of darkness below ground.

Through my rear-view mirror I watched it sailing downhill until it smacked into a pleasant-looking bunch of trolleys who were having a quiet smoke and a natter down by the neatly kept bushes.

They made a space for him and he settled in among them, rubbing shoulders with them, one of the gang again. I smiled and pulled out into the main road. I love a happy ending.

Chapter Six

I had spent the whole morning at my desk, trying to lose an extra six minutes out of my screenplay in order to accommodate the commercial breaks.

When I recorded *Lost for Words* for the audio version it weighed in at just over seven hours' reading time. I had already pared that down to one hour and twenty minutes by being brutal and cutting both of my kids out of the story.

'Sorry, kids, you're out.'

'Well, stuff you then.'

Actually they took it very well and I did manage to work in a reference to them so that the television audience would at least know they existed.

Now I cut that out as well, but I had to extend the part of my mother's cat Whisky, and so I was back to square one.

'I've left my mother's cat in.'

'Well, we know where we stand now, don't we?'

At least I had managed to sit at my desk for almost three hours without interruption and that for me was fast approaching a personal best, even if I still wasn't getting anywhere.

I always manage a wry smile when I hear authors saying that they cut themselves off from the real world by taking an office away from home, or that they work to a strict timetable. They should try fitting in their literary endeavours with cooking three and a half meals a day, doing all the shopping and picking their wife up whenever she falls over one of the cats.

I sometimes think the cats do it on purpose.

'Let's get him out of that office – go and trip Aileen up.'

'Why does it always have to be me? I did it yesterday.'

I must admit though that I rather welcome the interruptions. Those golden moments when the intercom buzzes and Aileen is on the other end.

'Can you help me? I've lost a stamp.'

When I pushed open her office door she was on her hands and knees under her desk, sweeping the floor with her fingers.

'I'm sorry to bother you but I've just licked a stamp and it's disappeared.'

She sat back on her heels so that I could investigate.

'Can you see it?'

'Yes, love.'

'Where is it?'

'It's stuck on the end of your nose.'

But so far this morning not a single interruption, and I was just beginning to feel like a proper writer when this rather small and, it must be said, incredibly stupid vole marched into my study, sat down on the hearthrug and began to polish his whiskers.

I don't know how he got in, but he certainly hadn't thought it through. This vole was not the sort of vole destined to explore the dizzy realms of higher education.

He certainly hadn't taken an 'O' level in survival techniques.

There were three cats in my office at the time of his arrival. Thermal was fast asleep on my desk, serving as combination paperweight and book-rest. Tigger was fast asleep on the fax machine, her tail tucked inside the paper guide, so that if I had needed to send a fax she would probably have gone along with it. William, for reasons known only to himself, was sitting in the fireplace, staring up the chimney. He has done that a lot recently. It's his new hobby. We have chimneys in practically every room and William has stared up them all – for hours on end. One day he will appear on *University Challenge.*

'*William Cat – reading chimneys.*'

I sat as still as I could, which is very still. I am extremely good at sitting still. I have been practising ever since I was a child. So had the vole apparently. Or maybe he was on some illegal substance. Whatever it was it certainly wasn't speed.

He sat on the hearthrug, inches away from William's tail, and inspected the quality of the weave. Not of William's tail – of the rug. It's Chinese and I am very fond of it. It's the only hearthrug that never leaves its post. All the others creep surreptitiously around the house during the night and have to be rounded up and sorted out next morning.

I thought about what to do next. If I made a move I would wake Thermal and Tigger. William would turn around and the vole would be history. What would David Attenborough do in a situation like this?

Well, if his past record is anything to go by he would nip behind the nearest bush and whisper sweet nothings into a microphone while the three cats tore the poor little devil to pieces, and I wasn't having that.

Tigger's glass water bowl was on the floor by my foot. The other two share a bowl in the kitchen, but Tigger refuses to share with anyone. She says it's unhygienic. She read it in a book somewhere.

Very slowly I bent down and picked up the bowl. I had filled it first thing this morning and now I needed to empty it. As quietly as I could I trickled the water into the waste-paper bin. It seemed to take for ever and sounded so loud that I was sure it would wake them up.

Thermal opened just the one eye and glared at me in disgust.

'For goodness' sake, man – use the litter tray.'

But Tigger woke up with a start and as she did a fax came through. This is always the highlight of her day. She jumped down and began to attack the paper for having the temerity to squeeze its way out of our machine.

William strolled over to let her know that he was there if she needed him and at that point the vole suddenly realized what a mess he'd got himself into.

He almost had kittens. Fortunately he ran over towards me to have them and as he hesitated for a moment, wondering how best to negotiate the north face of my desk, I dropped the glass bowl over the top of him.

The fax was forgotten. Tigger and William raced over to see what was going on and Thermal leaped off the desk to join them.

I must say I was rather impressed with myself and I was even more impressed with the vole when I joined the cats and studied him at close hand.

Distorted by the thick glass, his head seemed to fill the entire bowl – it looked enormous. He snarled and the cats backed away. It was the first time they had seen a sabre-toothed vole.

'*What the hell is it?*'

'*I've no idea, but don't get too close.*'

I slipped a clipboard under the bowl and carried him down the stairs to the courtyard, where I let him go. But he just sat on the step and stared at the empty milk bottles for a moment or so and then began to smarten up his whiskers once again.

'Go on. Get out of here.'

He was making a really good job of his whiskers and I wondered how he managed to keep them looking so bright and shiny without the aid of an expensive conditioner.

'Push off.'

But he wasn't your 'wash and go' type of vole. He took his time and he took a lot of trouble. He didn't know the meaning of split ends and dandruff. In fact he didn't seem to know the meaning of anything very much and he was just about to start plucking his eyebrows when Patrick yelled at me through the hedge.

The vole was off like a shot. One minute he was quietly considering the possibility of adding the odd highlight here and there and the next he was well on his way to breaking the land speed record for voles with learning difficulties.

I know how he felt. He's a good man is Patrick, but the power of his voice always startles me. I think it's to do with his being Irish and their long history of large families. As a kid you have to shout to be heard and it never leaves you. Bridie, from across the back lane, doesn't need to ring the doorbell. We can hear her muttering to herself as she walks across the courtyard, and when Kealen, who is one of eleven, has a coffee with us in the kitchen, the pan lids quiver with every word she utters.

Even so, Patrick takes some beating and the privet hedge winced as his voice whistled through the leaves.

'Are you there, Deric?'

'Yes.'

'I can't hear you.'

That's the trouble with us one-off kids. We don't speak up. I shouted that yes, I was there and then retreated into the small hallway off the kitchen where his dulcet tones wouldn't ricochet off the four garden walls. He told me that the police had just rung to say they had recovered the stone balls from the gateposts. They were bringing them up for us to identify that afternoon.

All through this conversation I ran in and out of the hallway, shouting out my replies and then diving for cover before Patrick could resume his assault. It was good news and I passed it on to Aileen before going to tell the cats.

Thermal was asleep on my desk, Tigger flat out on the fax machine and William staring up the chimney. I think I might get a pet vole. They are much more fun.

That afternoon I was due in Leeds, at the Yorkshire Television studios, for a session with the producer of the play, Sita Williams, together with Alan J. W. Bell, who was to be the director.

I wondered what to wear. Writers are supposed to look wild and dangerous, so I spent some time staring into the depths of my wardrobe. You may have seen those literary pundits on late night television, looking for all the world as though they have come to the studio straight out of bed, hair in a frenzy and wearing clothes that would have looked more at home selling copies of the *Big Issue*.

Well this artistic image doesn't just happen. It takes time to look as scruffy as that, you have to work at it, and it takes even longer to look wild and dangerous. It took me ages and I failed miserably. I looked more like the vole I had rescued earlier on. We both had that vulnerable air about us, as if we cared too much what other people thought. So I decided to go for the lovable look instead.

The blue jacket with the brown shoes suggested that perhaps there was just the merest hint of the rebel hidden in there somewhere and I contented myself with the thought that I could always look wild and dangerous next time, when I wasn't in so much of a rush.

In fact the only rebel on duty at that moment was my right sock. I suppose on any other day it might just as easily have been my left sock, but today it had been randomly chosen as my right sock and there was something not quite right about it.

It seemed to be all ruckled up under the sole of my foot and try as I might I couldn't sort it out. So I changed my socks and still the right foot was just as uncomfortable, wrinkled up as though it was frowning. Perhaps it was the shoe that was causing the trouble.

So I changed my shoes and still the right foot was acting up, just as grumpy as ever. It was like walking across a freshly ploughed field. So I took off both my shoes and my socks and embarked on a barefoot hike across the bedroom carpet.

Perhaps it was the carpet? I had a go in the bathroom where the floor covering is as smooth as a bowling green and still my right foot felt as though it had recently been corrugated.

It must be the foot itself. I ran my hand over the length of my bare sole and I couldn't feel anything wrong with it, so I lay flat on the floor and, with the help of the magnifying mirror balanced on the edge of the bath, tried to make out what the trouble was.

Then Aileen came in and fell right over the top of me and while we were lying there, side by side, on the bathroom floor, we discussed feet.

'Do you ever feel as though one of your feet has been corrugated while the other one is perfectly all right?'

'No.'

It wasn't a long discussion and it solved absolutely nothing at all, but I felt a lot better when she said that I looked very smart indeed and sounded as though she really meant it.

Some people wouldn't take too much notice of a blind woman's opinion but I do, mainly because I love her and trust her and also because I become very desperate at times.

I also left her to identify the stone balls when the police arrived that afternoon, so I had no idea what might be waiting for me when I arrived home.

The Yorkshire Television studios in Leeds look as television studios ought to look and that isn't always the case. There are those that could easily be mistaken for a potted meat factory, but here in Leeds a vast reception area leaves you in no doubt whatsoever.

Waves of contestants for *The Price is Right* or *Countdown* gather on settees under enormous photographs of Bruce Forsyth and Richard Whiteley. David Jason, thinly disguised as Frost, stares across the room at a vast trophy cabinet, while over at the yuppie-free reception desk they somehow manage not to sound patronizing as they deal with people like me.

I had hung around outside, waiting for the automatic doors to spring open, and it wasn't until someone came barging through from the other side that I realized they weren't automatic at all. You had to push them. I could only imagine what I must have looked like from the reception desk.

Man in blue jacket and brown shoes stands outside building and waits patiently for a moment or two, giving the double doors plenty of time to acknowledge his presence. When they don't he waves his hand uncertainly from side to side in a vain attempt to attract their attention before taking a couple of paces backwards, and then he approaches once more, this time in what he imagines to be a more confident manner. The doors continue to ignore him, and so he tries a little jump in the air to see if that will do the trick. It doesn't, and he stands there looking puzzled and forlorn until a man he believes he once saw doing strange things to a sheep in *Emmerdale* barges through from the other side.

It's all very sad. Some deep-rooted politeness gene always insists that I say thank you to automatic doors as they let me in or out, just as I never fail to thank that rather pleasant woman who operates the speaking clock, together with her colleague who so efficiently manages the 1471 service all on her own.

'You were called today at 14.30 – the caller withheld their number.'

'Thank you.'

I thanked the doors anyway, just to be on the safe side, and passed embarrassedly through reception on my way to the meeting.

Sita and Alan were waiting for me and after a quick cup of coffee we settled down to work. Over the past few weeks Sita and I had met several times in her office at the Granada studios in Manchester and I found her to be warm and witty and hugely experienced, with a long list of credits to her name. We had already gone through

78

the play scene by scene and I admired her and liked her a lot.

Now we were about to go through it line by line and this can be a soul destroying business for the writer. Up until now the plaudits had come thick and fast. All those concerned at Yorkshire Television had told me that I had something very special and for weeks now I had gone around with a great big smile on my face.

They loved it, they said, but the fact that they had budgeted the best part of a million pounds on a single drama was the greatest compliment of all.

Selling a single play to television these days is no task for the faint-hearted, especially if that play is singularly lacking in cops and robbers. We didn't have a handsome young vet and nobody took their clothes off. There were no car chases, no lesbian love scenes and nobody got shot. We did have a doctor, several nurses and a couple of hospitals, but then you can't change the world overnight.

Alan Bell started the ball rolling on page two.

'Do we need that line?'

'Yes.'

'Why?'

'Er . . .'

I couldn't for the life of me think why we needed that line. I couldn't even remember having written it. As a writer I am a marathon runner rather than a sprinter and I needed to lie on the floor in a darkened room for a while, think about it, have a bath, turn it over in my mind and then sleep on it.

They wanted answers right now and they were spinning off each other.

'What about scene nine?'

'*What* about scene nine?'

'Do we need it?'

I slipped slowly from the settee and sat on the floor. I tried to look intelligent, making notes in my unreadable handwriting as the two of them unravelled my play like some lousy piece of knitting. They must know what they were talking about, they'd done it all before.

Then as the afternoon wore on we started putting bits back in. We did need that line and scene nine proved to be absolutely essential and I began to realize that I had written a pretty tight script after all.

Sita and Alan were throwing ideas about and some of them were very good indeed, but they were freshly plucked ideas and needed work and I had laboured on this play for six solid months.

By the time Keith Richardson, the head of drama at Yorkshire Television, joined us, my fragile self-confidence had perked up a little and I was making notes I could almost read, which was a great improvement.

Then Sue Jackson, the casting director, popped her head round the door and spoke to Keith.

'Pete Postlethwaite says yes, he'll do it.'

A broad smile crept across Keith's face and the two of them discussed money for a while, then they upped it and Sue went off to clinch the deal. Sita was very excited and so was I, even though I had never heard of him.

'He's wonderful. Haven't you seen *Brassed Off*?'

'No.'

'*Sharpe*?'

'No.'

I think I was a bit of a disappointment to them. Later on I learned that Alan Bell didn't know much about him either but he had been bright enough to keep his mouth shut.

Alan Bell is probably best known as the director of the BBC comedy *Last of the Summer Wine* and we'd had lunch together with Keith a week or so before at Alan's club in London.

As we stepped into the club foyer an attendant had barred my way.

'Sorry, sir.'

I wasn't wearing a tie and they wouldn't let me in until I had sorted one out from a selection they kept in a shoebox under the counter at reception.

I picked the sort of tie that instantly marks the wearer out as having either been educated at Eton or spent several years as an officer in the Guards, and yet as I knotted it round my neck it was patently obvious to anyone with half an eye open that I was more likely to have attended the Manor secondary modern school in Chesterfield and gone on to serve as a senior aircraftsman in the RAF at Hereford.

'Looks very smart, sir.'

I couldn't understand why they'd let Keith in. He was certainly wearing a tie, but then he wears them so loosely slung that it's hard to tell whether they are supposed to be round his neck or helping to keep his trousers up.

Alan looked the part until he took his overcoat off and it was discovered that he wasn't wearing a jacket underneath.

'Sorry, sir.'

The powers that be wouldn't let him into the dining room of his own club until he found one and they didn't keep a selection of jackets in their shoebox.

So Keith and I took our seats at a table in the dining room and talked about him as we worked our way through the best part of a bottle of wine until, some twenty minutes later, he arrived, wearing an ill-fitting jacket he had torn off the back of one of the lavatory attendants.

'Looks very smart, sir.'

It was fashioned out of royal blue nylon, with the bright yellow logo of the cleaning company stamped large across the left breast pocket. It fitted where it touched and was humming with static electricity, but all was well with the world. He was wearing a jacket and that was what mattered. Strange places, these London clubs.

It was well into the evening before Sita, Alan, Keith and I hammered out the closing sequence. The leading character, my mother – played by Thora Hird – had already died in hospital before the end of the play but I wanted her to have the final word in voice-over.

'*I'm going nowhere without my teeth.*'

I had fought hard for the line and I seemed to have won. Sita went off to find someone who could give her a docket for the taxi back to Manchester and Alan headed off towards his hotel. Keith, who doesn't seem to have a home to go to, sat back in his chair and smoked his umpteenth cigarette of the day.

I was very lucky that the play had finished up in his hands. He had fought like mad to get it networked, he believed in it completely, and now he had Pete Postlethwaite. Keith was the sort of man you needed on your side in this business and he smoked even more than I did. What more could anyone want?

On the way home I called in at the video shop and the woman disappeared among the display racks to find me a copy of *Brassed Off*. It didn't take her long.

'Have you seen it before?'

She was staring down at me from behind the counter as I sat on the floor and tried to sort out my corrugated sock.

'No, I haven't.'

'Oh, you'll love it. Pete Postlethwaite is absolutely brilliant.'

And he was. I didn't even wait to put the car away. I parked up by the side gate and rushed in to watch the film with Aileen. We laughed and cried and then watched the film all over again as we ate our dinner. While Pete was on the screen you couldn't take your eyes off him, and he had some stiff opposition.

We shed real tears as he lay in a hospital bed and the brass band played 'Danny Boy' from down on the lawn beneath his window and we cheered his rousing speech in the Albert Hall. We even gave him a round of applause as the credits rolled and I can't remember ever clapping the television before.

Then we replayed the bits and pieces we had especially loved before sitting back with what was now an early morning cup of coffee.

'Just think. He's going to be playing me.'

Aileen smiled and stroked my hand.

'Yes. And you've got your balls back as well.'

I had forgotten my balls.

'Are they all right?'

'Yes. The police put them in the garage, down the right-hand wall so you can still get the car in.'

I had forgotten about the car as well and it was pitch black outside. I switched on the headlights and a stray cat stood mesmerized for a moment as I pulled into the garage. I wanted to tell him about the cellar where he could get a warm bed for the night and a hot breakfast first thing in the morning, but he quickly pulled himself together and was gone.

And so were the balls. Not a sign of them. Someone had nipped into the garage and pinched them while we were watching the film.

Chapter Seven

I could have taken the ring road and given Chesterfield a miss but I don't get too many opportunities to drive around my childhood haunts. Even though the town is changing at a rate of knots, it still holds many memories for me.

I checked my watch. Half an hour and I must be off. Just time to have a look at the old house in Heaton Street where I was born and from there it's only a hop, step and a jump along Old Road and then a sharp left into Storrs Road.

My mother didn't travel very far. Four houses from birth to death and all of them within the same square mile. It makes life very convenient when you are taking a trip down memory lane.

I pulled up across the road from number forty-three and switched off the engine. It was here in 1936 that my mother had been dragged away from a card game at midnight and rushed off to hospital in Bob Pearson's van. She hadn't wanted to go, she was winning and she had a good hand, but I had insisted on being born.

They say I hung on until she had made it to the foot of the hospital staircase before making my first

84

appearance. I wasn't a difficult birth. I couldn't wait to get out into the big wide world and apparently my dad was very proud of me that day, probably for the first and last time in his life.

My mother and I went to hospital together not so very long ago, a year or so before she died, and she asked if we might drive down Heaton Street so that she could have a look at the old house. I had pulled up on this very spot and for the umpteenth time she told me that the little garden wall had once sprouted iron railings.

I remembered them well. My father painted them a couple of times a week. He would always have a drop of paint left over from his latest job and it seemed a pity to waste it.

For three days they would be jet black with silver knobs and then I would come home from school to find they had magically turned olive green with brown and gold knobs. They were his pride and joy, until one day the powers that be came to cut them down.

'It's because of the war. They are going to make guns out of them.'

My father was heartbroken. I remember my mother trying to make him feel better, while I sat in the corner and tried to imagine the British Army going over the top, firing cardinal-red guns with big gold knobs on the end.

As my mother and I sat there a lady with lilac hair came hobbling round the corner of Rhodesia Road. I can't remember her name, but I do remember that over the years her hair had changed colour about as often as our railings.

She recognized my mother and came over to have a word with her. In fact she managed to have several thousand words before my mother was able to grab an opening and butt in. In the meantime I almost hypnotized myself by staring at her pale pink scalp as it shimmered in the sunlight through the thin lilac covering.

At last the woman made the mistake of asking a question, which was where my mother entered into the conversation.

'What are you doing down here, then?'

'I just thought I'd stop and have a look. I'm going in hospital to have an operation.'

We then had ten solid minutes of my mother's medical history, ranging from that dreadful time in her schooldays when they thought she would never pull through, to the moment a fortnight ago when she came over all peculiar and had to lie down.

'Are you going private?'

'No, of course not.'

My mother seemed surprised at being asked such a stupid question.

'Deric's coming with me.'

I cruised slowly along Old Road, past the little shop at the top of St Thomas's Street. My mother was still calling it Hooley's, I think it was, long after Mr Drury had taken the business over. Then when Mr Drury retired after ten years or so and sold it on, she immediately decided to start calling it Drury's. She was always one owner behind and it didn't really matter until she came over all sophisticated and acquired one of those newfangled chequebooks. The new owner took it in his stride, waiting until she'd left the shop before crossing out the name Drury, inserting his own, and then forging her initials in order to make it all legal and above board.

*　　*　　*

The half-hour was ticking by, so I wasn't able to spend much time on the other two houses. The fourth, where my mother first saw the light of day, had been pulled down long ago and the site was now part of the grammar school playing fields.

A week ago a team from Yorkshire Television had covered this same route, taking notes and photographs of her last two homes so that they could recreate the interiors in the studio back in Leeds.

I waved to an old neighbour of my mother's who stopped weeding long enough to wave back and wonder who the hell I was, and then I set off for Matlock, where I was to talk to a mass meeting of mobile librarians.

They were coming from all over the country in their library vans and I had an awful vision of having to stand in the middle of a field and shout at them through a megaphone. But no, they were going to park up and then hold a series of meetings in the Derbyshire County Council offices. I was to be the light entertainment after lunch and I was quite looking forward to it.

In her later years my mother was a great supporter of the Derbyshire mobile library service.

'I don't know what I would do without them.'

She never took out a book in her life, but the librarian on her route very kindly agreed to ripen her green tomatoes on his dashboard as he drove around the county and she thought he was absolutely wonderful.

'I always give him half a dozen for his trouble.'

I thought they were absolutely wonderful too. They had all the vans lined up in the car park, getting on for fifty or so, some more or less what you would expect, others the last word in sophistication, with lifts for the disabled and playing areas for the children.

I did a tour of them all and tried to pretend I wasn't hurt when they didn't have copies of my books on board.

Librarians have it made when it comes to dealing with authors. If your books are on the shelves they take you straight to them.

'There you are.'

If they don't stock them, have never stocked them and wouldn't even dream of wasting their money on them, they smile and lie in their back teeth.

'You're very popular. Your books are always out. We've got a waiting list as long as your arm.'

The conference drew to a close and the vans began their long journey home, to the South Coast, the West Country, some having only to pop over the Pennines, others taking the tortuous route back to East Anglia. They left the car park in a constant stream, one after the other, heading for the M1, and passers-by stood with their mouths open at the sight.

'I don't know. You wait for hours for the mobile library and then thirty-seven come along all at once.'

I followed them for a while and then, on impulse, doubled back to have another look at Matlock. One of the first things I came across was a large photograph of myself in the window of the Firs Bookshop.

I took it in my stride. Hardly glanced at it. One gets used to these things after a while. Just a quick sideways peep to make sure they had my hair colouring right and that the smile was winsome enough and yet not over the top.

I was just trying to remember what on earth had happened to that shirt I was wearing and whatever possessed me to buy it in the first place when I smashed into the rear of the car that had just pulled up short in front of me.

The driver was out of his seat in a flash. He was one hell of a size and he sort of unfolded out of his Volvo like a well-oiled action man. He was wearing a pair of those camouflage trousers that are designed to make you almost invisible in the jungle but don't half stand out when they are advancing towards you in the middle of Matlock town centre.

From his number one haircut right down to his big black boots he was road rage incarnate, and he was tapping out a tattoo on my window. I pressed a little black button and the passenger window immediately eased its way down.

I stared at him through the glass for a moment and then pressed another button and the driver's window gaped open. A bullet-shaped head came through and joined me in the car.

'Are you all right?'

His voice was gentle and concerned. I had thought as I watched him striding towards me that I might fake a broken rib or two – a little simulated whiplash right now might save me a great deal of pain in the long run. But he seemed genuinely concerned about me, his face as troubled as a face can be when it's topped off with a haircut like that.

'I'm fine, thank you.'

'Are you sure?'

'Yes, really.'

His face broke into a great big grin and his haircut panicked and hung on for dear life.

'Let's have a look at your car then, shall we? See what the damage is.'

I had come off worst. He had one of those towbars sticking out from the back of his car, the sort they use for pulling caravans, and it had buried itself deep into my bumper, with the result that both ends had flirted off and my car now looked as though it was wearing a droopy moustache.

His Volvo was comparatively unscathed. His towbar had buckled slightly and his bumper had a cute little dimple that might look rather attractive in a certain light.

'I'm sorry. I can't think what I was playing at.'

'Ah, don't worry about it. I can knock that out in a few minutes.'

We decided to leave it at that. What with the excess on the insurance it wasn't worth the trouble of claiming. I apologized again but he wouldn't hear of it.

'Life's too short,' he said.

We shook hands and he went his way and I went mine. My way was backwards, into a vacant parking space. The bumper was now dragging on the road, and so I yanked it off and slung it over the back of the empty seat, one end in the passenger well.

A man who had been watching us closely during all this came over to have a word with me.

'If you want a witness . . .'

'How do you mean?'

'He never even looked. Backing into you like that.'

'He what?'

We leaned against the car together, my photograph smirking at me from the bookshop window as he explained.

'He was reversing into here.' The man kicked my car tyre to show me what he meant by here. 'Never even looked to see if there were owt coming up behind him.'

My witness scribbled his name and address on the

back of an envelope and went on his way. I jumped in the car and the bumper gave me a warm welcome and then belted me across the left ear. I screwed up the envelope and dropped it in the passenger well. What the hell. Life's too short, isn't it?

Back at home there was a tape recorder waiting for me on the kitchen table. At that moment I would have given anything to see instead a great big steak and kidney pie with new potatoes, green beans and one or two sprigs of that long thin broccoli that seems to be all the rage down at Marks and Spencer's nowadays.

It would be nice to come home to a piping hot meal once in a while, I thought, instead of having to roll up my sleeves and start from scratch. But then I switched on the tape recorder and heard Aileen's lovely voice and knew I would rather come home to her any day of the week.

'Guess what. Helen's got the afternoon off from the surgery, so she's picked me up and we've gone shopping. I'll be back about half-past six because she's on call tonight. Hope your day went well. Love you.'

So she would be in capable hands. Our doctor has a good eye when it comes to a bargain. She helps Aileen with the colours and the sizes and is always ready to offer that all-important slice of psychology.

'Of course you can afford it.'

She would also be on hand with expert medical advice when Aileen ruptured herself hauling her carrier bags out into the car park.

I extracted the wok from the cupboard and began to chop up a chicken, a couple of cloves of garlic, ginger, spring onions, peppers, celery, sweetcorn. That's the trouble with Chinese cooking, it's all stir-fried in a couple of minutes – as long as you've spent a couple of hours on the preparation beforehand.

The chefs on television have it all too easy. The ingredients to hand in bite-sized bowls, minced by minions and laid out in the correct order. Not a pot to wash and not a single cat in sight. They ought to try it in our house. A studio audience would be a doddle after cooking for years in the presence of four critical cats.

'Oh hell. He's getting the wok out again.'

Aileen bought me the wok for Christmas, together with a stainless steel cleaver and hardwood board. For my birthday she bought me an asparagus steamer. She really knows how to spoil a guy.

The cats hate to see the wok come creeping out of the cupboard. They know the bottle of soy sauce is likely to follow hard on its heels and they can't stand soy sauce at any price.

'He'll ruin that chicken.'

They can't stand the sizzling and spitting either. What was wrong with the good old-fashioned beef and two veg? Done in the oven as God intended. You knew where you were with that.

In the old days they would sit, two of them either side of our chairs, looking up appealingly, catching odd bits of rogue beef in mid air. Every now and then a lump of coarse horseradish would slip through the security net and have them flat on their backs, coughing fit for their lungs to burst. But it was a small price to pay and the offending morsel could always be rinsed under the tap and then you could hardly tell the difference.

Best of all were the scrapings from the meat dish, together with the leftovers and surplus gravy. That was really living. But have you ever tried licking out a wok? No wonder those Siamese cats always look as though they've just eaten something that didn't agree with them.

But the cats brightened up considerably when they saw the prawns I had bought to go with the avocado.

'*He doesn't muck about with them.*'

I had to muck about with the avocado. It was as hard as a rock and I should have left well alone, but it had lain in the fruit bowl for over a week now and I just assumed it would be ready for eating.

The cats moved in for a closer look. All except Tigger, who wouldn't dream of doing anything so vulgar. She stayed aloof, sitting with her paws buttoned up tight together, over by the fire in the corner.

The avocado took the edge off my cleaver as I sliced it in half and then I had the job of removing the stone. It was as though it had been set in concrete. I stuck a knife in and wiggled it about, but this one was going to need major surgery.

I dug deep and twisted hard and the stone shot out like a bullet. It flew across the kitchen, clipped the ceiling light and then dropped like – well, like an avocado stone, I suppose.

Tigger was minding her own business, filing that claw on her left paw, the one that's always given her trouble, ever since she was a kitten. She was just slipping the claw back into its sheath when the avocado stone smashed down on the top of her head.

The effect, as they say in the adverts, was shattering. Her legs folded up underneath her and she fell over and got up, only to fall over again, and then she staggered about on the kitchen tiles like a heifer in an abattoir.

I picked her up and her eyes rolled and she seemed to pass out. I didn't know what to do. The kiss of life perhaps?

'*Where am I?*'

She played the scene to perfection. It was just like an old movie. She even gave a polite cough to suggest there might be a hint of consumption.

I took her up to my office together with half a dozen prawns. You would be amazed at the healing properties half a dozen prawns possess. They ought to be on prescription.

After a while she curled up in my chair and fell fast asleep. It's not really allowed during the day, but there were special circumstances and Tigger is not one to let a special circumstance go by without giving it her full attention.

The noise downstairs was horrendous as three small cats belted an avocado stone around four skirting boards. If ever an avocado stone paid for its sins, this one did.

It was my fault really. Fancy starting off a Chinese meal with avocado and prawns. Ken Hom would ask for his wok back if he ever found out. I replaced the two halves in the fruit bowl to give them a chance to ripen and then picked up the colander in which I had rinsed the prawns.

Empty. Not a single one left. I looked round accusingly at the cats. Thermal was over the other side of the kitchen. He had the avocado stone trapped under the table and his rear end swayed from side to side as he moved in for the kill.

William, who should have been acting as his right-hand man, had been sidetracked. He does tend to get sidetracked, does William. He was staring closely at a tiny spider who had decided to climb up on top of the biscuit barrel. William doesn't know it's rude to stare and the spider was beginning to realize that coming up here probably hadn't been such a good career move after all.

Little Chap was sitting over by the breadbin, licking his lips and washing his face. He strolled over to join me and sat down by the colander.

'*Any more of those? They were very pleasant. Made a nice change.*'

He was a very happy little chap indeed, until I shouted at him. His sense of belonging is still paper thin and he just went to pieces.

They tell me that out in the park he's known as the Lion King. Large dogs think twice before taking him on and then don't. One that thought twice and then did was still licking his wounds a couple of weeks later and has since developed a nervous twitch that turns into an all-enveloping shudder whenever he approaches the park gates.

But here in the house Little Chap has found himself a bolt-hole. No need to be aggressive or to sleep with one eye open, he can crash out wherever he chooses and be perfectly safe. Everybody is pleasant to him and food is delivered at regular intervals, on saucers and on time, and if he feels like a snack in between meals he has only to throw back his head and holler:

'*Fooooood.*'

And now he'd gone and done something terribly wrong and blown it all. He knew he would eventually – he always did. He wondered what it was he'd done this time and he couldn't think of anything, but that nice man was shouting at him so it must be something very serious.

Instead of making a break for it he simply gave himself up, laid his chin on the draining board and tensed his abject little body, miserably waiting for the inevitable blow to fall.

I patted him on the head and found him a small prawn that had got itself wedged in a hole in the colander. He stared at my peace offering for a moment, thinking it might be a trap, and then began to chew it in slow motion as I lowered him to the floor.

William shouted at him to come and have a look at his spider and I picked up my cleaver and set about a red pepper. Well, life's too short, isn't it?

Chapter Eight

The birds woke me even earlier than usual this morning. I think the tall one has a cold. His voice seemed huskier than before and his heart wasn't in it. He had managed to cough his way through only the first few bars of Rossini's *Barber of Seville* before the short one cut in with his latest mobile phone impression. He has been practising Call Waiting for some time and he's just about got it right. The tall one seemed quite happy to hand over the reins and I took a sip of last night's whisky and water and huddled under the duvet, listening as the short one went on and on.

Last night's whisky doesn't taste quite the same in the early hours of the morning and I needed a cup of coffee. Aileen stirred beside me, unduveted and naked as the day she was born, but in much better shape. I sat up and admired her various curves and curlicues for some time until she shivered gently and reached for the duvet.

I covered her and eased myself out of bed. The short one had turned round and was staring in at me through the rooflight, so I automatically pulled in my stomach and puffed out my chest and then felt rather daft. I thought for a moment that I might dial 1471, ring him straight back and tell him to bugger off, but in the end I decided to ignore him and go and make that cup of coffee instead.

The cats decided to ignore *me* as I pushed open my study door. Backlit by the light from the hall I must have cut a ghostly figure as I crept, cup and saucer in hand, towards the table in the window. Tigger opened just the one eye and then quickly closed it again.

'Don't look, chaps. He's stark naked.'

Thermal decided to chance a peep. After all these years he still hasn't worked out how I do it. He'd love to be able to strip off every now and then, on hot summer days and after he's slept too long by the radiator. He spends hours searching his undercarriage, looking for the zip, but so far he hasn't found a thing. That's not quite true – he has found a thing, but he's still looking for the zip.

He came over and joined me at the table and we stared out across the park together. There were lights cutting through the dark, dozens of them, pinpricks at first, strobing through the trees, then growing in stature as they came closer.

Thermal was transfixed. He sat on the table with his back to me, staring out of the window, every muscle on red alert, his two little ears standing to attention, framing the scene for me like a couple of bookends.

I tried to make out what was going on. What looked like a huge spaceship emerged from the gloom, then came to rest in the centre of the park. It was as though I were sitting in on the opening sequence of *ET*.

'ET go home.'

'Pardon?'

'It was a movie. The hero had a look of you about him.'

'*Did he?*'

Thermal preened at the thought. I hope to God he's not around the next time they show the film on television.

A flotilla of smaller craft began to surround the mother ship. There must have been over fifty of them, and then as the daylight began to thread its way through the trees and the mist decided it had better things to do with its time, a splash of red and gold lettering solved the mystery.

The Moscow State Circus was with us once more and raring to go as usual. They don't hang about. As Thermal and I sat idly drinking our coffee, me from my cup and Thermal from my saucer, an enormous marquee was raised higher and higher until it was as tall as my house and able to look down on the trees.

Dozens of caravans huddled close round and a series of smaller tents rose as though they had been instantly inflated. A generator burst into life and the marquee suddenly filled with light, turning the sombre dark wine of the canvas into a vivid scarlet red.

By six in the morning everything was in place, as though it had always been there. A strongman emerged from one of the caravans wearing only a pair of underpants that he had obviously borrowed from a much smaller man. He attached a hosepipe to a temporary cold water tap and waited while the water decided to shift itself.

Thermal and I shivered at the thought and then the strongman's rather stunning young assistant joined him, wearing an even smaller pair of pants and a bra so tiny that at first I thought she had it on back to front.

The water eventually decided to appear and the two performers shared a bar of soap as they hosed each other down in a scene that was wonderfully erotic for six o'clock in the morning. Thermal wasn't all that impressed, but then he didn't have the binoculars.

'How about a spot of breakfast?'

'*Just the two of us?*'

'Yes. Be like old times.'

Silently we crept from the room. Past William, who was flat on his back and snoring gently, fast asleep on the hearth so that he would be in position for chimney duty the moment he woke up. Past Tigger, who had both of her front paws draped over my Compaq laptop, her head resting neatly on the disk drive.

Past Little Chap, who normally preferred to sleep in the cellar, but who had Velcroed himself to the radiator for the night in order to extract every last drop of warmth. Had it been switched on he would have really felt the benefit.

They don't all four usually sleep together like this. Must have had an important meeting last night. Maybe it had dragged on and on and they'd had a few drinks and decided to stay the night. I would ask Thermal about it over breakfast. I like to be one step ahead.

But first I had to read aloud a selection of interesting bits from the *Daily Telegraph*. This is a service I once provided exclusively for Aileen's benefit, but over the years Thermal has become used to hearing me drone on over the breakfast table and so as soon as he has had a perfunctory nibble at his saucer of tuna chunks he comes over and leans heavily against my ankle, listening intently. Even though Aileen was still fast asleep in bed I had to give him at least a taste of the ritual before he would even think about going out in the courtyard for his early morning run.

Huddersfield Town football club were top of Division One for the first time since I moved here and the Pope had apologized for the behaviour of all the other Popes before him. It's becoming all the rage, this apologizing for the sins of our forefathers, and I can't help thinking it's rather silly. It means absolutely nothing, except to a handful of politically correct halfwits, and I strongly object to the government apologizing on my behalf for the behaviour of my ancestors in days gone by.

I wasn't there, it wasn't me, I didn't do it and what's more my great-uncle Jack, who was there, didn't know any better at the time. Before long the powers that be will be insisting that Florence Nightingale's descendants apologize for her not having used penicillin during the Crimean War and King Alfred's lot will be forced to apologize for that time when he burned the cakes, especially to those who were unfortunate enough to get lots of little black bits stuck between their teeth.

I can get quite heated about these things but Thermal wasn't interested. I can tell by the way he purrs. He ticks over for most of the time, it's become a habit with him. Even when he's fast asleep he sounds like a well-bred getaway car parked round the back of the Midland Bank – a Mercedes or a Jaguar XJS or some such model that has been regularly serviced at a properly appointed garage.

But the moment his interest is aroused he steps on the gas and his 4.2 engine leaps into action, rattling a fading bodywork that would feel much more at home on an elderly Citroën 2CV.

I combed through the paper, from the front page to the business section, where I paused for a moment, marvelling at how the *Daily Telegraph* manages to fit in so many photographs of attractive young women among its rather dull reports of the doings of the CBI and Alan Sugar. There were five of them today. Three posing with a mobile phone, one smiling and not looking where

101

she was going while driving a car and a financial adviser who was wearing an ultra-short skirt, stiletto heels and a rather supercilious expression. Then I found the sort of thing I was looking for.

'Listen to this, Thermal.'

His ears tuned in to the excitement in my voice and his paw hovered over the accelerator pedal in anticipation.

'It says here that over two thirds of the world's production of Benedictine is drunk in the pubs and clubs of Burnley.'

Well, you could have knocked him down with a feather. It shook me, I can tell you – it's not often you come across a piece of vital information like that in the newspapers. They are usually packed full of the more trivial stuff such as the greenhouse effect, world recession and pink being the new black.

'Just think of it, Thermal. We live within spitting distance of the place where they drink more Benedictine than anywhere else in the world.'

He thought about it as he went back and sorted through the massed ranks of tuna in his saucer. He knows I slip a vitamin tablet in among the chunks every morning and his first avowed intent is to find and destroy it before it can do him any good.

I read on. Apparently during the First World War a battalion of Lancashire soldiers known as the Burnley Pals were camped near the Benedictine monastery in France and immediately fell in love with the sickly sweet liqueur that the monks turned out in such huge quantities. It kept out the cold, they found, and made the war seem that much shorter, so after the conflict was over they made sure that they took a plentiful supply back home to Burnley with them.

And the tradition lives on to this day. Burnley is the

only place where the drink is sold upside down with the other optics. The Plumbe Street Miners' Working Men's Club stocks Benedictine in three and a half litre bottles and the Plumbe Street Miners' working men knock it back as if there was no tomorrow, in hot water or with lots of ice, as the mood takes them.

I felt intensely proud of Burnley, just as I did when I found out that here in Huddersfield we eat more sliced pickled beetroot than almost any other place on earth.

But Thermal wasn't paying attention. The vitamin pill was proving an elusive little devil and he knew from past experience that the only way to deal with it effectively was physically to get in there among the tuna chunks and sort it out.

So he took a deep breath and plunged in at the shallow end, coming up for air every now and then as he trawled his way through the murky depths. I must get him a snorkel and a spear gun; at least he'll look more professional.

In the meantime I ripped open a packet of cold comfort capsules I'd bought from Boots the chemists. I had a busy week ahead, the highlight of which was to be the first read-through of the play, and I couldn't risk the streaming eyes and running nose that I knew were well on the way.

I suffer from a cold more than anyone else in the world. I have worked on with a broken arm, a broken leg and a broken collarbone, but a common cold immediately puts me out of action and leaves me walking around like a zombie, with my eyes streaming and my brain bouncing around my skull like a boxer on the ropes.

I flipped a couple of capsules out through the foil

backing and glanced at the leaflet to see how many I should take.

Two capsules to be taken with a drink every four hours up to a maximum of four doses in twenty-four hours.

Simple enough. I could handle that. I washed down the first two capsules with the remains of last night's whisky and took another glance at the leaflet to pass the time. Apparently there could be side effects on occasion and I read through the list as I tried to get rid of the rogue capsule that had become stuck to the back of my throat.

Stomach pain, sputum retention, nausea, vomiting, diarrhoea or constipation . . .

Diarrhoea *or* constipation? My God. They were versatile little devils, these capsules.

. . . headache, blurred vision, ringing in the ears, irritability, sleep disturbance, loss of appetite, difficulty in passing urine . . .

I didn't think I would have any difficulty in that direction. I was almost wetting myself right now.

. . . rapid heart rate, shaking, skin rashes and sweating.

I glanced down at my bare chest. There did seem to be a small rash, just to one side of the single hair that has begun to look quite distinguished since it turned a steely grey. But it wasn't all that easy to tell. What with the rapid heartbeat, the shaking and the sweating it wouldn't stand still long enough for me to form an educated opinion.

The list wound up with a mind-boggling get-out clause.

If concerned . . .

Concerned? I'm frightened to death.

. . . or if anything else unusual happens . . .

Anything else unusual? The only things they haven't

mentioned so far are gangrene, ectopic pregnancy and rigor mortis.

. . . *talk to your pharmacist* . . .

And a lot of good that would do. I knew exactly what Chris Holt, my regular pharmacist, would say.

'And what the hell were you doing in Boots anyway?'

'I was just passing.'

'No. That's what you should have done. Where you went wrong is you went inside and bought something, so don't come round here looking for sympathy.'

I shuddered at the thought, but then Thermal brought me swiftly back to the here and now. He'd found the vitamin pill. He always does – I don't know why I bother hiding them.

His whiskers trembled with disgust as he rolled it around his mouth a couple of times before spitting it out like a bullet. It smacked hard against the fridge door, rebounded, spun round a couple of times, then circumnavigated the fringe on the circular rug like a drunk on his way home from the pub before tottering over towards the pedal bin, where it collapsed belly up on the floor. Thermal stood up, had a good long satisfying stretch, and then gave the vitamin pill a sharp clip round the earhole as he passed it on his way out of the back door.

I didn't really know what to do with the day. No more script changes until we started shooting and then it would be a case of rewrites on the hoof. Tomorrow I would be in Leeds for the read-through of *Lost for Words*. The entire cast, a crew of some fifty hardened professionals, the director, producer and executive producers, would all be there along with Aileen and myself.

The thought of being trapped in a room while the actors spoke my words for the very first time was both frightening and intensely exhilarating. A book is very much a private affair. I'm never there when the reader decides to skip a couple of pages or puts it down in disgust. I can kid myself that they savoured every word, laughed like a drain and cried their eyes out, and then went straight back to the beginning and started all over again. But tomorrow there would be no escape. I would be able to hear the disdain in the actors' voices, watch the despair in their eyes as they exchanged desperate glances with one another:

'How did I get myself mixed up in this load of old rubbish?'

'Oh what the hell – at least it's a job.'

Simon Gray once described the art of the playwright as an unnatural pursuit and he had it dead to rights. I was thinking I might end it all and leave a suicide note on Aileen's tape recorder when the kitchen door opened and in she came, hair rumpled with sleep, staring in vain at something she had clasped in her hand.

'I trod on this on the stairs. What is it – a penny?'

She pushed a small coin under my nose.

'No, love. It's a five-pence piece.'

Her face lit up.

'Oh goody.'

And off she went to pop it in her purse, in the compartment she reserves for fives, tens and twenties. What a nice start to the day. Hardly out of bed and she was already fourpence to the good. I felt a surge of love run right through me and decided to put off committing suicide for the time being and put on the kettle instead.

The five-penny piece also reminded me of a change I had had to make in the script. We had brought the story up to date, which would save a lot of trouble. Only twelve years had passed since my mother's death, but in that short time an awful lot had happened.

We would have needed a fleet of twelve-year-old cars, with the appropriate number plates, and the cameraman would have had to avoid shooting any passing traffic. Satellite dishes would have had to be removed and road signs checked against a twelve-year-old highway code.

In such a short time the nurses' uniforms would have evolved along with the everyday clothing of the cast. The beer on sale in the pub, television sets, kettles, newspapers, books – costumes and props would have had to check everything.

They have to do it all the time of course, but it would be much easier to bring the action up to date. It wouldn't make a scrap of difference to the story so that's what we had done. The only flaw in the script was that my mother's house was still priced at £19,000, so I popped up to my study and with a few taps on the computer keyboard I whipped the value up to £45,000, and then I sat back and rather wished I'd held on to it for another twelve years.

I had passed William and Little Chap on the stairs as I went up to my study. They came charging round the first bend in harness, then split at the last minute, one either side of me, before skidding to a halt on the second landing.

'*What about breakfast then?*'

'Shan't be a minute.'

That wasn't what they had wanted to hear and William gave a deep sigh and settled down for the duration. Little Chap decided to fill in the time by having a good scratch.

Tigger had still been fast asleep on my laptop, so I

lifted her head from the disk drive and gently slid her little body over towards the printer. She isn't getting any younger, and beneath her silky hair I could feel the hard knots that the dreaded arthritis has been busily weaving in her flanks.

Every morning I give her a full body massage. I work my thumbs slowly over her shoulders and then down the length of her spine before bringing my fingers into play on her stiff little haunches. It's become something of a ritual and it's usually about a quarter of an hour before she decides that enough is enough and I am dismissed until the same time tomorrow.

When we reached the kitchen Thermal had returned from his early morning stroll and had joined the other two in their noisy demand for a full English breakfast.

'*Fooo-oood.*'

It looked like Bakewell cattle market in there, with Aileen stranded in the middle of the floor, not daring to move in case she trod on the three indignant little bodies that milled around her feet.

I led her safely to the table and sat her down with tea, toast and marmalade.

'*She always gets served first.*'

'*She sleeps with him, you know.*'

'*That accounts for it then.*'

I fed the cats, Thermal for the second time in an hour, and as soon as they had sorted out what was what and whose was whose I left them to it and went over to the park for a closer look at the circus.

The tap-dancing squirrel was already up and dressed and perched on the very end of a slim branch that bobbed gently under his weight as he surveyed the tented village. As a kid he had often dreamed of running away to join the circus and now a circus had run away and joined him. Happy days.

The big top dominated the scene and I peeped in through a flap and watched as a well-organized team filled the vast space with a stage, seats and scaffolding, shouting at one another in at least seven different languages.

Outside the smaller tents and caravans, ancient and modern, were more people, all of them loudly eloquent in foreign tongues you don't come across all that often in Huddersfield. Scouting about ahead of me were two young girls, about fourteen or fifteen I would guess, on their way to Greenhead College and speaking in a tongue that you don't often come across in Moscow.

'Ow about us comin' here tonight?'

'We can't afford it.'

'We can, we've got six pound twenty between us.'

'No, we haven't.'

'Yes, we have.'

'No, we haven't. I've got five pound twenty and you've got a quid.'

'That's the same thing.'

'Oh no it isn't.'

''Tis.'

''Tisn't.'

They carried on their way, still debating their financial situation, and I wondered where they would be in ten years' time. The one who was hanging on to her money would probably be a high flyer with the Halifax Building Society while the one who was trying to screw it out of her would be making a small fortune on the Monday open market.

It must have been thirty years or more since I last walked round a circus. That was back in Chesterfield, at Stand Road, Whittington, where Roberts Brothers came once a year and fly-posted the town.

I would have had Sally and Nick with me, one hanging on to each hand, buzzing with excitement as we walked round the animal cages after the show. There were lions and tigers, Arab stallions and a moth-eaten old camel who would spit at you if you came too close. There would have been elephants and monkeys and donkeys and performing seals and that's what was missing here in Greenhead Park.

Not an animal in sight. It's for the best, I know. I have never felt comfortable watching the poor beasts being put through their paces on my behalf, and yet as the human performers limbered up outside their tents and tended to their equipment the atmosphere just wasn't the same. Too antiseptic. More like a gymnasts' convention than a circus.

And then I spotted one of our four-legged friends. Not one of the big cats and certainly not a wild cat, but more than welcome nevertheless.

Little Chap high-stepped his way across the damp turf, stopping dead in his tracks every now and then to sniff the air and listen. He's an absolute poser when it comes to sniffing and listening. He likes to give the impression that he's a direct descendant of an old Red Indian guide cat who could pick out a buffalo at thirty miles. His ears swivel in all directions and he sticks his nose up in the air to such an extent that he looks more like a direct descendant of Kenneth Williams.

For what seemed like ages he stood there, balancing on three legs, his right front paw hanging limply in mid air, suggesting that his Indian role model had been as queer as a coot. Then he hopped over a couple of guy ropes and slipped silently down on to his stomach as he scrambled under the rear of a small tent.

Almost immediately he came out through the front door, this time draped lovingly over the shoulder of the young woman I had seen taking an impromptu shower earlier in the morning. She was wearing a thin robe and probably little else and she took him over to introduce him to her partner, who was lifting weights by the side of their caravan.

I had a vision of Little Chap ending his days in Vladivostok, so I nipped over to explain that he was my cat and that I lived over there. I pointed to Little Chap, working my way through the age-old pantomime routine that we always bring out when we are talking to those poor unfortunates who are not able to speak our language. I tapped myself on the chest and pointed over towards my house.

'My cat – lives over there.'

I think they understood. They patted him and they stroked him and whispered sweet nothings in his ear. Little Chap was enchanted. He hitched himself higher and higher until his paws were hanging down the woman's slim back and his head nestled beneath her long blond hair.

'*Take no notice, madam. I have never seen this man before in my life.*'

Chapter Nine

I had forgotten that I was supposed to take the car in for a service, but Perry's made it easy for me. They insisted on driving us to the railway station because it looked like rain and promised to have the car ready for when we got back from Leeds.

I quite like taking the car in for a service. I have a chat with everybody and then tour the showroom, sitting in brand new Jaguars that I can't afford, revelling in the smell of wood and leather. Then I have a cup of coffee and read the *Yorkshire Post* and if it's raining somebody takes me home.

Far cry from the old days when Jim Swallow, God bless him, kept my ancient Lancia alive, with a mixture of old-fashioned expertise, a collection of second-hand bits and pieces and the odd prayer here and there.

Picking it up afterwards is a different story. Perry's bill always comes to about twice as much as I paid for my first car, but then Sharon smiles at me from behind her desk and it seems well worth every penny. On the way home the car purrs with pleasure and all the ash-trays have been emptied and I want to carry on until I reach Edinburgh.

The train was going to be late, the announcer told us, in a wonderful accent that had started out in a Barbados kindergarten and then come over here to a finishing school in Huddersfield. Ten minutes approximately, he said.

Not really long enough to walk down to the waiting room for a cup of tea and so Aileen and I settled ourselves on a bench and waited. After a minute or so a young man joined us and sat down next to Aileen.

He had a mobile phone stuck to his left ear and he seemed to be waiting for someone to come to the phone at the other end, so he just sat there, not saying a word. Aileen smiled at him and he smiled back.

Then he sat up straight, uncrossed his legs and spoke into his phone.

'I'm going to miss my appointment.'

Aileen turned towards him.

'Oh, I am sorry. It should only be about ten minutes. That's what they said on the tannoy. Maybe they'll make it up.'

The man glanced at her and carried on with his phone call.

'Could you do me a favour?'

'If I can,' answered Aileen helpfully.

The man inched away from her, along the seat. He hadn't far to inch. About an inch or so, I would guess. I tapped her on the arm to gain her attention. She shook me off – she was talking.

The young man had the phone tucked into his chest by now and was almost whispering.

'Any chance you could ring them for me?'

Aileen was only too happy to oblige. She reached into her handbag and took out her mobile phone.

'Here. You can do it yourself. Just dial the number

113

and then press the top left-hand button.'

She was about to hand it over when the man stood up and wandered across to the newspaper stand. Aileen watched him go in amazement. How rude!

'He wasn't talking to you, love. He was on his mobile. You couldn't see it.'

She flushed with embarrassment. She hates it when she misjudges a situation.

'Why didn't you say something?'

'I tried.'

Twenty minutes later the train still hadn't arrived and the young man came over once again, hovering uncertainly in front of the bench.

'Could you do me a favour?'

Aileen looked at me for help. History was repeating itself. But before I could say anything the young man went on.

'Could I take you up on your offer, only my phone's gone dead and I haven't any change?'

Once more she dipped into her handbag and offered her phone, this time explaining why she had made the mistake. He apologized profusely and said there was no way you could tell. He moved out of earshot while he made his call and afterwards came and sat down and they chatted away together as though they had known each other for years.

I borrowed his *Daily Mail* and shared the next few minutes with Lynda Lee Potter. I know when I'm not wanted.

In Leeds he walked with us as far as the Queen's Hotel and then excused himself, racing off through the traffic towards the ever-growing business district with its clutch of buildings, ancient and modern, that have amazingly embraced each other like old friends.

The newfangled brick melts in with the old-fashioned stone in a way that I would never have thought possible. The new kids on the block have about a week to flex their muscles and show off their charms before yet another boy wonder rises from the dust, to take over and catch the eye in a space that one never noticed was there in the first place.

The beauty of these buildings must come as quite a surprise to some first-time visitors, especially those who have decanted from the M62 on to the M621 and then made for the Dark Arches and Granary Wharf. As they swing around the left-hand bend on their way towards the Hilton Hotel they will have cut their sightseeing teeth on a miserable Portakabin of a building, squatting on a piece of unkempt land behind a tatty old fence. A sign will tell them that this is the home of the Leeds College of Architecture.

It always reminds me of a plumber I know, whose wife can't get him to mend the leaking tap in the bathroom.

Thank goodness the Queen's Hotel can't see it. This is one of those wonderful old railway hotels. Some aren't looking so wonderful these days, but the Queen's remains as solid as ever. Hugely impressive but not at all pretentious, like one of the old Yorkshire wool barons – rich as Croesus, but can't be doing with any fuss.

We had a little time on our hands, and so we popped inside, settled down with a large pot of coffee and snuggled up together on a deep, comfy settee. I produced the *Daily Telegraph* from the soft leather briefcase that I had bought for Aileen's birthday and then stolen off her a week later.

I took out my pen and folded the newspaper in half and then half again, so that we could get a clear run at the crossword.

The man opposite leaned towards us across the small table and waited, motionless, until he was sure we had noticed that he was leaning towards us across the small table, waiting, motionless.

'Tell you something you won't know.'

'What's that?'

He produced his own copy of the *Daily Telegraph* and laid it on the table, facing the back page towards us so that we could see what he was on about.

'The quick crossword. The answers to the first two clues always make a phrase or a saying when you put them together.'

Aileen leaned forward, across the table, towards the voice.

'Yes. My favourite was "De Gaulle" and "keeper".'

The man's face fell.

'You know about it then.'

Aileen hadn't seen his face fall.

'Yes. This morning it's "lettuce" and "pray".'

The man snatched up his paper.

'Bugger. I haven't even had chance to look at it yet.'

So, having completely ruined his day, we finished our coffee, said a fond farewell and headed off in a taxi towards the Yorkshire Television Centre in Woodhouse Lane.

The place was packed and at first I thought we must be late, but a glance at my watch told me that we had made it with a few minutes to spare. There were eighty-odd people milling around, fifty or more from the production side along with a cast of over twenty actors, all of them drinking coffee or fruit juice and looking very much at home.

Aileen instinctively moved towards the buzz of conversation. I tightened my grip on her arm and held her back.

'Would you like to go to the toilet before we go in?'

'No. I'm fine.'

She took a step forwards and I yanked her back.

'Let me put it another way. I'm going to the toilet, are you coming?'

She thought about it for a split second.

'Yes. I think I desperately need to go to the toilet.'

We found a his and a hers. She went into hers and I went into his. I lit a cigarette and leaned against a radiator.

What had I started? All the money involved and all those people out there. Soon they would be reading my lines and there would be only one person to blame for a script that didn't quite stand up – the writer.

Thora Hird had just completed a play by Alan Bennett and Pete Postlethwaite was being courted by all the big names in America. Who the hell did I think I was, exposing my soul like this? It would be like walking naked down Regent Street.

The door opened and Aileen strode in.

'Ready?'

There was a rustling noise from one of the cubicles. The sort of rustling noise you make when you are minding your own business, sitting on a toilet seat in a gents public lavatory and you suddenly hear a woman's voice. I put my fingers to my lips and whispered:

'You shouldn't be in here.'

'Neither should you. Come on – let's get cracking.'

I stubbed out my cigarette in a tinfoil ashtray that had

117

gone a long way past its retirement date. It winced and went a funny shape.

'I'm terrified.'

Aileen came over and settled herself on the radiator.

'Look. Thora loves it – she has done from the start.'

'I know but . . .'

'And Pete Postlethwaite can pick and choose his parts as he likes. He chose this.'

'Yes but . . .'

'Keith Richardson thinks it's wonderful and so does Alan Bell. They wouldn't be doing it otherwise.'

In the cubicle a plastic seat shifted slightly and then a toilet roll began to whirl merrily around, as they do when you are trying not to make a noise.

I took a deep breath.

'OK. You're right. Let's get going.'

Aileen gave me a kiss on the cheek as I opened the door for her and then, as it slowly closed behind me, a broad Yorkshire voice rang out from behind the cubicle door.

'Good luck.'

As it happens we didn't need any. We slipped unnoticed into the throng and helped ourselves to coffee. Gales of laughter swept over from the far corner where a small crowd was gathered in a circle, heads bowed as though they were admiring the pattern on the carpet.

'Thora's over in the corner.'

Aileen and I have taken her out on many an occasion. Leave her alone for a couple of minutes and you have to fight through a whole army of well-wishers to get back to her side. She's like a magnet. Once, in a very smart restaurant, the waiters spent a good half-hour waving starters, main courses and puddings under unresponding noses, in a vain attempt to entice the other diners back to their tables.

'She's very approachable, isn't she?'

'Yes – but I think she'd like to start her soup now.'

Today she was in her element. Holding court in her wheelchair, surrounded by her fellow professionals, she was telling them how she was first carried on stage when only a few weeks old. Over the next month she would bring the story up to date. Only eighty-six years to go.

I had been looking forward to meeting Pete Postlethwaite and he was just as I had wanted him to be. Down to earth, no nonsense and as far from a luvvy as you can get.

Some years ago I was introduced to one of my celluloid heroes, a man who specialized in tough northern roles. I had watched him on television for years, playing hard-bitten policemen, jobbing builders, that sort of thing – if you wanted a bluff town councillor, honest to a fault, here was your man.

And there he sat, poncing about on a settee in Brown's Hotel, holding a china cup between thumb and forefinger, little finger pointing at the ceiling while he wittered on about how he had always been miscast, in a voice like Donald Sinden on speed.

But Pete could have walked straight from the set of *Brassed Off*. He has the most wonderful face, with cheekbones as high as those of an American Indian. Someone once said that they weren't cheekbones at all – they were shoulder blades that had been put in the wrong place.

Penny Downie, from the National Theatre, was to be Aileen for the next thirty days or so. It was a smaller part than she was used to playing but she had seen something in the role and wanted to do it. She and

Aileen were huddled together, sitting at a small table in another corner. They were getting on like a house on fire.

Someone offered Aileen a cigarette that was a little shorter than the brand she normally smoked. She lit it about half an inch away from the end and was then very surprised to find that it wasn't working. She tried to light it again, and once more it failed to function. Penny guided her hand towards the cigarette and we had lift-off. Here endeth the first lesson.

It's much easier for actors to play fictional characters. They can flesh them out and make them their own, but real people bring along extra baggage with them and this has to be sorted and sifted until a fine balance is achieved.

The blindness was going to be a problem for Penny. We have all seen actresses stumbling about in B movies, arms flailing out in front of them like punch-drunk boxers. More recently I saw one who had the arms just about right, but who moved hesitantly through the film as though, underneath her crinoline skirt, she had filled her nappy about a fortnight ago and it was now hanging down around her knees.

Keith Richardson called us all together, settled us down and introduced us to one another, and then the read-through began. I am not very good at names, but voices stay with me for ever and as the story unfolded many of them became flesh.

As the chemist I heard Norris, Derek Baldwin's salesman sidekick from *Coronation Street*, played by Malcolm Hebden. The mother from the comedy series *Watching* came to life as the wonderful Noreen Kershaw played the part of Margaret.

Coronation Street reared its head once more as Anne

Reid read Gloria. She left the show years ago, but to a lifelong fan like me the voices of the past never fade. These days I can enjoy her in Victoria Wood's *Dinner Ladies.*

Director Alan Bell took notes but I just listened and it wasn't half as painful as I thought it would be. Three quarters of an hour later it was all over. We'd had some good belly laughs, the odd gulp whenever Pete and Thora handled one of the sadder moments and a smattering of applause at the end.

During the reading we had seen our two main characters come together as mother and son. They were getting on well, and although Thora had all the best lines, Pete didn't mind. His job was to be the catalyst, to hold the whole thing together, and he had done it wonderfully well considering that he was playing the part of a rather boring man.

Afterwards Thora went straight to work recording voice-overs with Alan Bell and David Whiteley, the sound recordist, while the rest of us took care of a cold buffet. Every now and then a head would pop round the adjoining door and bawl at us.

'Shut up.'

We would shut up and listen as Thora strutted her stuff.

'*Do you want to be buried, Mum – or do you want to be cremated?*'

'*Oh I don't know, love. Surprise me.*'

Thora was to keep working at a cracking pace throughout the shooting of the film, a punishing schedule that would have taken it out of a much younger woman. She was on set first thing in the morning and still at it late in the day, even though there were times when she was not at all well.

Everyone fell in love with her and she loved being involved. Even on her one day off, when we all expected her to have a lie-in and recharge her batteries, she arrived on the set well before breakfast.

'Do you mind if I watch?'

She hates not being in the thick of it. She just loves company, and after a gruelling day's work she would grab the make-up people, the dressers or anyone she thought would be good value for money and take them out to dinner at the noisiest Italian restaurant in town. Then, back in the Marriott Hotel, she would work on her lines, before waking Pete in the early hours of the next morning.

'Are you going to take me down for breakfast or what?'

Meanwhile Penny was still keeping an observant eye on Aileen. Pete had insisted on escorting my wife to the toilet.

'I'll wait and take you back.'

'Don't worry. I know the way now.'

So he'd left her to it. She memorizes every step and takes great pride in being independent. We watched her negotiate her way back through a pair of double doors and then tentatively ease her way down a wooden ramp, feeling for the handrail.

Penny watched her every step, making mental notes, while I remembered a New Year's party at the home of our friends Alison and Paul. We had left about two in the morning. Others had stayed on.

The next morning a couple arrived to collect their car.

'I did enjoy talking to that redhead last night. You know – the author.'

'Yes,' said Alison. 'Didn't she do well, considering that it's not her house.'

She was greeted with a blank look.

'How do you mean?'

'She's registered blind.'

'Well, I'll be blowed. I had no idea. I saw people offering her a hand, telling her what the food was on the table, filling her plate and all that, but I thought she was just pissed like the rest of us.'

We spoiled ourselves and took a taxi back to Huddersfield. I have a problem with taxi drivers – I need to talk to them. I find it physically impossible to sit in the back of a black cab and ignore the person who's doing all the work. They probably just want to sit there and think beautiful thoughts but stuff that, I have my needs and I need to talk.

Of course it doesn't help when the taxi driver hails from one of the more remote villages of Pakistan and I can understand only one word in every twenty-five he utters – it doesn't make for a meaningful exchange of ideas.

As far as I could tell, this one was having trouble with his daughter and that worried me. I watched a television programme not long ago and apparently, in the more isolated regions of Pakistan, they have their own way of dealing with troublesome daughters. They beat them to death.

Maybe I had it all wrong. I thought he had asked me if I had any children. It threw me for a moment because I had just asked him whether he was starting his shift or about to finish it. Anyway I told him I had one of each.

'A son and a daughter.'

I was about to add that I also had four stepchildren, but the word daughter launched him into a diatribe that lasted for almost half an hour, until he pointed at the sign for Huddersfield at junction 24 on the M62.

'No – the next one.'

And he was off again. The muscles on his neck stood out in knots and his face in the rear-view mirror seemed contorted with uncontrolled anger. Maybe he was just telling me that it was no business of mine whether he was starting his shift or finishing it, or that his daughter had just qualified as a doctor and he was very proud of her.

But I doubt it. Aileen said afterwards that maybe it was simply his natural way of expressing himself, but there was more to it than that and it disturbed me. I wanted to be able to find out if I was right or wrong but his machine-gun delivery continued to defeat me and he was still at it as we pulled into the back lane.

William was sitting in the gutter, staring down the grate, and I pointed him out to the driver and asked if he would be careful not to run over him. He pulled the taxi to a halt within a foot of William's backside. Whether he'd understood what I'd said I shall never know. He had his daughter on his mind. I know she was on mine.

I paid him and off he went, still muttering to himself. Aileen marched up the path with her front-door key stuck out in front of her. She gave a little jump in the air and all the outside lights came on. I must have the electronic eye lowered.

I went over to William and told him to come in. He gave me a look which told me to push off.

William is into grates. Just as in the house he spends most of his time peering up the chimney, listening to the birds as they warm their bums on the chimney pot, once outside he spends hours and hours peering down the grate in the back lane.

He once spotted a small rodent and the thrill has

124

stayed with him ever since. He sits in the gutter, still as a garden gnome, head bent in total concentration as visiting cars try to manoeuvre round him, parking almost on his tail.

Every now and then he springs into action, his paw diving down through the bars as he sees something moving in the murky depths. I have done a few basic sums and reckon that since his front legs are roughly six inches long and the grating is some four feet deep, whatever lives down there is more than likely to die of old age. They probably think he's waving to them.

'He seems a very friendly cat. Must go up there and have a chat with him some time.'

Aileen and I sat and drank coffee, discussing how the read-through had gone at Yorkshire Television. There had been a feeling about the place that we had something special. Everyone had read the script beforehand and they were even more enthusiastic now that a little life had been breathed into the pages.

We talked it over for an hour or so and then I went up to my study and came back into the real world, to phone my daughter Sally in Brighton, to see if she was happy and to tell her I loved her.

Chapter Ten

I should have known it was going to be one of those days. I had set it aside as a writing day, no interruptions. Aileen was going to field the phone for me but it burst into life long before she surfaced.

Paul Wolfenden is a lot like me. He has to share things and if there's no one else around he shares them with me, on the phone. We were once a double act and when you have died on stage together as often as we have you form a bond which allows you not to worry whether the other one is awake or not.

I can hardly remember a thing he said. I was busy juicing two grapefruits and a conference pear at the time. I love my juicer. Aileen bought it. I said we didn't need it, but now I don't know how we managed without it all these years.

I added a kiwi fruit. I had never juiced a kiwi fruit before and Thermal sat hypnotized as a rather unhealthy-looking green liquid came dripping out of the other end. Tigger is frightened of the juicer – she's frightened of anything that you have to plug in and switch on – so she sat out in the hall, peeping round the door. William had popped out to check on his drain, and so it was just me and Thermal and Paul on the phone.

He told me several jokes, but I can only remember the last one. I can only ever remember the last one anyone tells me. I'm very bad at remembering jokes.

'I said, "I like your perfume." She said, "Yes, it's a new one. It's called Tester." '

Paul said that perhaps I might be able to use it in a book. I said no, I couldn't do that – it would be cheating.

He rang off. He's a busy man and he had lots of other people to annoy, so Thermal and I settled down to our breakfast of rabbit and chicken in jelly and a bowl of crunchy nut cornflakes. I had the crunchy nut cornflakes.

Tigger put her head round the door.

'*Have you finished with that thing?*'

'Yes, come on in.'

She had a sniff at the rabbit and chicken in jelly and her eyes watered. It does pong a bit. Aileen can't bear to be in the same room and Tigger is allergic to it.

I fixed her up with a saucer of last night's left-over leg of pork and went back to my cornflakes. Thermal was outraged.

'*Excuse me!*'

'Sorry.'

I filled him a saucer of pork, all cut up into tiny chunks, and added a dollop of sage and onion stuffing to make him feel wanted.

'*I should think so.*'

We ate in silence, until Tigger produced one of her Walker's barbecued beef and onion crisps from in between the Japanese tea cups. She shared it with Thermal and they crunched away in stereo until the back door bell went berserk and had both of them hiding behind the rubber plant in the far corner.

We have had a stand-in postman for the last couple of weeks or so, while our regular is away on holiday. This one seems averse to shoving things through the letter box and always rings the bell. At first I thought it a rather charming way of introducing himself, especially when he told me that he had bought one of my books for his father.

'Last Christmas that was. But I don't think he's even opened it yet. He doesn't read as much these days – not since he went deaf.'

I was going to ask him to elaborate on that but then decided to let it pass as there are more productive ways of going mad. Since that first day he has had me out of the shower and running down three flights of stairs on more than one occasion. He must be under the impression that I spend the whole day wearing nothing more than a bath towel.

'He reminds me a lot of Gandhi.'

Today, however, I was fully dressed and it took him by surprise.

'On your way out, are you?'

'No. I'm working.'

'Where's that then?'

'Here.'

'What at?'

'Writing.'

'Oh. You're still dabbling then.'

He handed me my mail, nothing larger than a sheet of A4, and I asked him if he wouldn't mind just shoving them through the letter box in future. His face fell and he trooped off across the courtyard, doing a passable impression of a wounded fawn.

'Miserable old sod, that one.'

I was once talking at a charity dinner, seated on the top table with a whole bunch of people I had never met before. *Diana's Story* had just been voted the most popular serial on Radio Four's *Woman's Hour* over the past fifty years and I was justifiably proud. I had beaten Tolstoy and Jane Austen into second and third place respectively. (Neither of them has rung to say well done. I couldn't be like that, it's not in my nature – it depends on the sort of person you are, I suppose.)

It was being repeated on the radio at the time and the lady on my right told me how much she was enjoying it. A solicitor on my left cleared his throat.

'Are you still dabbling with the writing then?'

'Yes. Are you still dabbling with the law?'

He was rather hurt and went to great lengths to explain that one didn't dabble with the law. It was a very serious business.

'It's not a hobby, you know.'

I was about to close the back door when something moved out from under the hedge by the rockery. It was probably the toughest-looking cat I have ever laid eyes on, and I've seen some belters in my time. We have one down the lane called Denton who's as hard as nails, and my mother once had a cat called Horace. He was short of one ear and one nostril when he first planted his bottom on my mother's back door step and she wondered whether she should take him in.

'Somebody must be missing him.'

I tried to imagine the sort of person who could possibly be missing Horace and failed miserably. My mother went to have a word with him.

'I think he's a bit deaf in his left ear.'

'He hasn't got a left ear.'

'He's got a lovely smile though.'

And he had. He also had great dignity, which is more than you could say for the monster who was now shambling his way towards me across the courtyard. He could have been mistaken for a rather dishevelled hyena.

My first thought was to lock all the doors and draw the curtains and pretend that Aileen and I had taken the cats and gone off to Cornwall for a fortnight.

We had plenty of food in the freezer and a huge stock of cat litter in the cellar. We had enough down there to sandblast the Town Hall twice over. We could hide until he had gone away and want for nothing.

And then I had another look at him. He was a big cat, there was no doubt about that. You could have thrown a saddle over him and entered him for the 2.30 at Chepstow.

But a second glance told me that all might not be well with him. His coat hung loosely about his body like a cape, as though he had tossed it carelessly over his shoulders on the way out of the house and not even bothered to do up the buttons.

As he settled down to a crouch, he took it in stages. First he thought about it for a while and then he seemed to be explaining to each limb exactly what was expected of them.

It was as though his legs had never done this before. As though they couldn't remember whether they were supposed to bend forwards or backwards and it was some time before they managed to arrange themselves neatly, tucked away underneath him and out of sight.

His shoulders stood out through his coat like the pommel on a hunting saddle and his eyes wouldn't meet mine. One thing was for sure – he could do with a good meal.

Back in the kitchen I picked up Thermal's half-empty

saucer of rabbit and chicken in jelly, topped it up from the tin and filled another saucer with milk. As I went out to feed him it occurred to me that perhaps I should have brought a whip and a chair along with me.

'*Easy now. Down, boy. Back – baaaack.*'

Close to, he looked enormous. Even with his bottom still glued to the stone flags he was taller than any two of mine put together.

'There you are, boy. Try that.'

He rose and lumbered towards me. Despite his obvious problems he was still an awesome creature. He had little tufts of hair sticking out of his ears. Did we have wild lynx in this country?

He came to a halt and sat down once more, a little way off, eyeing the two dishes suspiciously.

'It's all right.'

He would be the judge of that. He'd been caught like this before. Once I was out of the way he would come and have a closer look.

I decided to leave him to it, but as I turned Tigger came striding out through the open door and made straight for the two dishes. First she gave the milk a proprietorial lick and then she made a brave attempt to nibble the chicken and rabbit.

The other cat slithered across the flagstones on his stomach like a sniper and I feared for her life. He'll tear her limb from limb, I thought. But then she has always had a remarkable way with other cats, however fearsome. Over the years she has sorted out any number of Thermal's enemies for him. Cats she can handle – you don't have to plug them in and switch them on. The old fellow seemed to recognize this and so he just plonked himself down by her side and waited patiently until she had completed the tests. She stood back.

'*I think you'll enjoy that.*'

'*Sure you've finished?*'

'*Please. Be my guest.*'

And with that he tucked in, the plate travelling along in front of him and across the courtyard. He came back for the milk and mopped it up with a tongue the size of a loofah, then looked around for more.

I emptied the remainder of the tin into the saucer and stood back, but the cat was still wary of me. Tigger reassured him.

'*It's all right. He's harmless.*'

He took her word for it and the food disappeared as though it had been thrown down a coal chute.

Tigger smiled indulgently.

'*Let me show you the accommodation.*'

And with that she escorted him down the cellar steps so that he could have a look round.

She was at it again. Mother Theresa was alive and well and living in Huddersfield. This was how we had acquired Arthur, William and Little Chap and enough was enough. I really didn't fancy turning the house into a hospice once again.

I followed them at a safe distance and peered in through the cellar window. Tigger jumped up on the cane chair with the Dunlopillo cushion and began to demonstrate its qualities.

'*I think you'll find it's very comfortable.*'

The newcomer thought about it for a while and then opted for the sheepskin blanket on top of the boiler.

'*Old bones, you know.*'

Tigger was most understanding. She waited until he had made himself comfortable and then, leaping up on to the old stone table so that she could watch over him, she settled herself down on a pair of my soft leather gardening gloves. They're very cosy – they've hardly been used.

A national newspaper had asked me to write seven hundred and fifty words on my mother, to be printed the week before *Lost for Words* was televised, and they were prepared to pay me in real money.

I rather liked the idea of being paid to write my own publicity, but it was proving to be hard going. I had already written about her in two of my books, in a television play, in more magazine articles and for more radio programmes than I care to remember. I didn't want to repeat myself. I wanted a fresh approach and so far I had run into a brick wall.

Bits and pieces of my life with her kept coming back to me, but not one of them had the legs to run to seven hundred and fifty words.

I remembered Betty Brothwood's, the chemist on Chatsworth Road in Chesterfield. She had a huge set of scales in the corner of the shop, especially for weighing babies, and they gleamed with brass. They were magnificent, as far removed from an ordinary set of scales as one of the old coach-built prams is from a modern pushchair.

The babies were laid on a pure white fluffy blanket, so as not to favour either sex, and Betty Brothwood herself would come out from the back of the shop and supervise the whole operation. I think it cost a penny.

But not for me. The butcher's at the end of Heaton Street was that bit nearer and a penny cheaper, so my mother would order a pound of stewing steak and half a pound of tomato sausage and ask them if they would mind weighing Deric for her while they were at it.

'*Give him up here then.*'

Not that I remembered of course. My uncle Len told me. He said that for the first eighteen months of my life I weighed in at one and sixpence a pound. What I do remember is making sure that a few weeks after my daughter Sally was born she was laid on the pure white blanket in Betty Brothwood's chemist's shop.

Several other fragments of my past offered themselves for consideration, but most of them were rather sad and not what was wanted at all, so I sat and stared at my laptop for all of an hour.

Aileen had gone out. Just after nine o'clock a car had arrived and whisked her away to North Yorkshire, to present the prizes at one of our few remaining grammar schools. So much for manning the phone – or the front door bell for that matter.

Compared with its mate on the back door, the front door bell is a proper little gentleman. It merely clears its throat a little and then enquires politely.

'Do excuse me, sir. I'm so sorry to bother you, but someone has just assaulted me with their forefinger. Do you wish to come down and have a word with them, or would you rather I simply gritted my teeth?'

However restrained its performance it has never yet failed to drag me out of the deepest coma and as usual I obeyed. When I pulled the door open there were three large women standing on the step.

'Sorry we're late, love. He forgot to pick us up.'

They didn't tell me who *he* was or who they were, they just pushed past me and hung their coats on the hall stand. Underneath they were wearing aprons and two of them had an armful of dusters and a bucket each full of aerosol sprays, while the third one dragged a chubby little vacuum cleaner behind her. It had a face painted on the front and reminded me of one of those things the council use for sucking out the drains.

It was the cleaning ladies from hell.

'I didn't know you were coming.'

If I had known, I would have been up there in North Yorkshire with Aileen.

'We told your wife one day this week – we couldn't be sure which. She said that would be all right.'

'Yes, well . . .'

To their credit they didn't muck about. They wore thick leather belts with holsters and they fired Pledge from the hip. Thermal had followed me some way behind and he was caught by a stray burst of Ajax Liquid the moment he put his head round the hall door.

'Sorry, puss.'

I picked him up and we stood back as this monstrous regiment of women moved into the lounge. They half closed the door behind them and then there followed a short pause before the radio burst into life, an expert hand whipping the dial through more stations than I ever knew existed before it came in to land on Radio Two.

Abba were about halfway though 'Waterloo' and it must have been some surprise to them when they were suddenly joined in harmony by three raucous voices and a badly tuned vacuum cleaner. They must have known they had competition because they immediately turned up the volume to the point where the brass lamp on the hall table began to have a fit and tried to throw itself over the edge.

Thermal and I were halfway up the stairs when William flew past us. He sat down on the first landing, breathing heavily. He was suffering from shock and smelled faintly of Pine disinfectant.

'It suits you, William.'

'*Thank you.*'

For the next five hours or so the three of us moved around the house like a pack of gypsies. At first we took refuge back in my study. Thermal opted for the peace, quiet and total stillness that can be found only in the bottom drawer of my desk. I yanked it open and he jumped inside. It's the deepest drawer and contains several translations of my books in German, Italian and Dutch. His likeness appears on all of the covers and I like to think he thumbs through them once I have shut him in.

William sat and stared up the chimney, listening to the cooing of the pigeons as they warmed their bottoms on the cowl at the top. I sat and stared at my computer, listening to the muffled snores that issued from the bottom drawer of my desk.

Apart from the distant drumming of the hoover down in the bowels of the house we had roughly an hour of peace and quiet before the cleaning ladies from hell began to climb the stairs, and very soon they had us surrounded once more.

They started off in Aileen's study before moving out into the hall and I listened to the bits and pieces of conversation that were shouted from one room to the other.

'I'm taking my own cakes – none of that bought rubbish.'

I thought of my mother's baking and of the days gone by when I would have given anything for her to have brought home a flip-top box, full of that bought rubbish from Henstock's.

'And I'm going to get a proper dress – one like those big dinner ladies wear.'

Long dresses, I finally worked out, the sort that posh ladies wear when they go to big dinner dances.

'It's not a cheap do. Mind you, talk about pricey, have you ever been to one of them motorway service stations? The prices! We set off early and stopped for breakfast. We had bacon, egg, sausage, tomato and fried bread, twice. The girl rang it up on the till and said how would you like to pay for it and my husband said how about monthly instalments.'

I was beginning to enjoy myself when the door burst open and the three of them charged in.

'Don't you worry, love. You won't know we're here.'

William had anticipated their coming. He must have smelt the Pine disinfectant as it worked its way across the landing and he'd just managed to squeeze himself down by the side of my walnut bookcase when he was caught by a badly aimed volley of Pledge, right behind the left ear. And if he's no better by this time next week I'm taking him for counselling.

I quickly unplugged my computer and tucked it under my arm. That's the advantage of having a laptop. In theory you can work anywhere.

In theory, that is. In practice I can't do anything of the sort. I set up my little box of tricks on the table in the dining room and stared at it for ten minutes, trying my best to look intelligent. I'm not very good at that either. A thought struck me, and I bounded up the stairs, one at a time, towards my office.

The women had completely cleared the decks. All my movable possessions were piled high on the long conference table in the window and they had somehow managed to tune my television set to Radio Two. I didn't know you could do that. Frank Ifield was belting out his once famous rendition of 'I Remember You'. It took me back because I remembered him, as it happens. It was like walking into a time warp.

One of the women was busily polishing my desk and I was instantly ashamed to see, from the virgin imprints, where my letter rack, table lamp and any manner of other bits and pieces had once stood amid the thick coating of fag ash and dust.

'Excuse me.'

'Of course, love.'

'Forgot something.'

I bent down and pulled open the deep bottom drawer, struggled a bit, and then plucked from it a small white cat who had gone absolutely rigid with fright. I tucked him under my left arm and with Thermal staring straight ahead, looking for all the world like one of those wrought-iron animals you might find stuck on the top of a weather vane in a Cotswold village, I marched confidently from the room.

Aileen rang to say that all had gone well. The head teacher had taken her out for lunch and there she had met an old schoolfriend. They were in the hotel now, chewing over old times and she would ring me later to tell me what time she would be home.

I didn't tell her about the invasion of the bleach people. They had gone through her study like a dose of salts and nothing would be quite where it should be. She needed to have everything to hand, where she could reach out, touch and find it, but we could sort that out when she came home.

'What's that noise?'

The vacuum cleaner had just clattered past my door on its way to the kitchen, which they had decided to leave to last.

'It's the television.'

'Don't forget your deadline.'

'I'll switch it off.'

I had pulled a hundred words from out of somewhere or other, read them through, and then tapped a key on the computer and despatched them to wherever it is they go when you tap that particular key. I didn't ever want to see them again.

There was another tap, this time on the window pane, so I moved the rubber plant to one side and saw Tigger, high on her hind legs, belting the living daylights out of the other side of the double glazing.

I had forgotten all about Tigger and her new-found friend in the cellar. I let her in and she let me know what she thought about me, in no uncertain terms. I couldn't quite make out what she said but the general gist of it seemed to veer towards my being inconsiderate, uncaring and idle soft.

Right, I thought. I'll show her who's uncaring. I stripped the last of the meat from the leg of pork and piled it high on a saucer. There was enough to have made a tasty supper for all three of them but we were talking Christian values here. The old cat down in the cellar deserved a break, so I filled another bowl with water and went off to give him a treat.

He hadn't moved, still fast asleep on the sheepskin blanket, even though I had barged in through the door and cursed under my breath when I cracked my knee on the Black and Decker workmate. I didn't want to wake him, no point in that, so I placed the two dishes on the floor where he couldn't fail to notice them and crept out as quietly as I could.

I was halfway up the stairs when something told me to go back and have another look at him. This time I padded softly across the stone floor and moved in as near as I dared. He was all curled up, with one paw wrapped around his face, covering his nose and both his eyes. It's a pose that always gets me. Thermal sleeps like that and he looks so cute, though I would never dream of telling him.

And so did this old fellow. With his tail tucked in between his back legs he seemed about half the size he was before and I was pleased he had found a safe haven where he would be warm and well fed.

I still didn't realize he was dead. He didn't look dead. Then I looked again. I felt his body and it was as warm as toast, but then he was lying on the boiler. I looked to see if there was any rise and fall in his body, but no, he wasn't breathing. I lifted his head and let it go and it fell down on to the blanket.

I sat for a while on the workmate and watched him, half expecting him to wake at any moment. At least he had had the comfort of a full belly and the warmth of the boiler.

There was a cardboard carton from Bibliophile Books on the floor, waiting to be torn up and tossed into the green wheelie bin. I picked him up and placed him in it. He fitted perfectly, so I closed the lid on him and went upstairs.

An hour later I took a spade and buried him in the little cardboard coffin, on the spare ground by the side of the house. Over the last sixty minutes his body had turned icy cold. At least the last few hours of his life had, in all probability, been far happier than much of what had gone before.

Back in the cellar I cleaned the spade and then trooped up the inside stairs to the ground floor. I had hardly known the cat but its death had affected me, leaving me flat and downcast, and so did the fact that the cleaning ladies from hell had called it a day and gone home, but not before locking the cellar door from the inside.

I banged and shouted for a while, but it was no use. They didn't have to wait for me to pay them, the agency sent a bill along later. They had probably thought I'd disappeared so that I wouldn't have to give them a tip.

'*He's a tight devil, that one.*'

So I began to clean out the cellar while I waited for Aileen to come home and a couple of hours later it fairly sparkled. But not nearly as brightly as my wife did as she told me about her day. Then I told her about mine and she laughed like a drain until I came to the bit about the stray cat.

I cooked us a meal and afterwards we had coffee while I read out loud a selection of edited highlights from the *Daily Telegraph*. The answers to the first two clues in the quick crossword were 'dupe' and 'hitter'.

Aileen decided to have an early night but I had to stay up and work on the article, even if it meant toiling away until daybreak. I stared at the blank screen for over an hour. My calculator told me that the going rate of pay worked out at fifty pence per word and of course the publicity would be worth its weight in gold.

Around two in the morning I was still staring at a blank screen and I knew that it wasn't going to get any better. So I flexed my fingers and typed three short words.

'Oh, sod it.'

And then I went off to bed. At least I had the satisfaction of having earned myself a steady one pound fifty, even if it was going to disappear down the drain when I pressed the delete key first thing in the morning. Ah, well. Easy come, easy go.

Chapter Eleven

One quick flip through the film schedule had told me that Thora wasn't going to have much time off for sightseeing. It would have been a punishing thirty-odd days for an eager young beginner still running on neat adrenaline, never mind a woman of eighty-seven who hadn't been looking at all well lately.

But there she was, on the set, in Clinton's card shop in Huddersfield, at half-past seven in the morning, having set off from the Marriott Hotel in Leeds at half-past six, before which she had already been given the once-over by the make-up artists and then fitted out in a bright green coat and red woolly hat by the dressers.

She looked rather frail as she sat in her wheelchair, thumbing through her script, mouthing the words quietly to herself. Shooting was to start with scenes sixty-seven and sixty-eight before the crew nipped smartly over to the other side of town to shoot two earlier scenes, numbers eight and nine.

Of course a film is always shot out of sequence, so whenever you read that an actor has *grown* into a role, it's more likely that they were in there to start with, then they grew out of it, grew back into it and then faded slightly in the early stages which were filmed later when they were beginning to wonder what the hell the movie was all about.

But Thora and Pete knew what it was all about and Alan Bell had the two-page scene wrapped up in no time at all. Thora had to be helped out of her wheelchair, but from the moment she was on her feet she became the consummate professional and immediately turned into my mother before my admiring eyes.

I had experienced the same feeling during the making of *Wide-Eyed and Legless* and nowadays, whenever I write about my mother, or even when I think back fondly to the old days, it's Thora's face that I see in my mind so that now and then I have to dig out some old photographs of my mother in order to hoist my memory back on to an even keel.

Nick and Sally have suffered from the same experience. As, inevitably, the mental picture of their mother fades somewhat, so the more they see Julie Walters in their mind's eye. It's all quite understandable, but nevertheless rather unnerving.

I slipped out through the shop doorway for a much needed cigarette. After the script is done and dusted the writer's role is very much on the edge of things.

I wanted to be there to make sure the feel of the script was coming over, and there would be the odd time when I would be needed to write a bridging scene, or to rewrite a few lines that weren't coming across as well as expected.

Ruth Holden, who was playing Nellie Elliot, had a line that needed watching closely. After she hears that my mother has had a stroke and that Mrs Corey is looking after her, she pushes past Pete with the words:

'That's *all* you need when you've had a stroke.'

Which tells us that she doesn't think much of Mrs Corey. Whereas with a slight change of emphasis –

'That's all you *need* when you've had a stroke.'

– she would tell us that as far as Nellie is concerned, Mrs Corey is up there alongside Florence Nightingale.

As I stuck the cigarette in my mouth a lighter was immediately shoved under my nose, from over my right shoulder, complete with half-cocked thumb.

'Thank you.'

I bent towards the lighter and an eight-inch sheet of flame shot up and singed both my eyebrows and that rather cute little curl that hangs down over my forehead on a good hair day.

'Sorry.'

The smell of burning was quite overpowering and I rubbed hard at my hair before I lost the lot. I turned and saw a man in a brown raincoat, tall and thin and completely without shoulders, like a telegraph pole. He was staring proudly at his cigarette lighter which he cupped fondly in his hand.

'Has a mind of its own, does this. You can't tell it a thing.'

I sniffed up at my eyebrows and they smelt awful, so I sniffed at them again, as you do.

'That's all right.'

He had a lump of cotton wool sticking out of his left ear. Not just any old lump of cotton wool, this was one of those huge wodges that you might find tucked in the top of a bottle of aspirins – the ones that keep on coming for ever and ever when you pull them out. It poked out of his ear and then hung down to where most people would have had a shoulder.

He nodded towards the shop.

144

'What they doing. Making an advert?'

'No – it's a film.'

He seemed disappointed, until he caught sight of Dame Thora through the window.

'I know her, don't I?'

'Thora Hird.'

'Oh aye. Now what is it that she's in?'

'*Last of the Summer Wine*?'

'That's it. And I know him and all, don't I?'

'Pete Postlethwaite.'

'Oh aye. Now what was it he was in then?'

'*Brassed Off*?'

'Oh aye. So what they doing here, then?'

'Making a film called *Lost for Words.*'

He thought for a while.

'Oh aye. I've seen that.'

'No. We're just filming it now.'

He nodded wisely.

'Ah well. It's all repeats these days, in't it.'

At that moment a smiling Thora came trundling through the shop door in her wheelchair and following hard on her wheels was her double, Dorothy Arnold, dressed in an identical coat and hat. The man in the raincoat swallowed hard as his eyes went from one to the other. A woman standing by his side nudged him.

'You were right about the repeats, love.'

I escaped back into the shop, but there was only the one way out and he was there waiting for me long after the film crew had left and I couldn't find an excuse for hanging about any longer. He seemed to have adopted me.

He stuck by my side until we reached the Midland Bank.

'I have to go in here.'

He came in with me, so I had to draw some money out of the machine that I didn't really need.

'Look, I really must be off.'

He walked with me as far as the car.

'When will it be on telly?'

'I'm not sure – around Christmas, I should think.'

We stood there, not knowing what to say.

'Hope your ear gets better.'

He tapped the cotton wool hanging like a dwarf's beard from his left ear.

'Oh this. A cotton-wool-bud-related incident, that was. Dangerous things, cotton-wool buds. Burst my eardrum.'

I loved the 'cotton-wool-bud-related incident'. It was like a Ministry of Health handout and it made the last half hour almost worthwhile.

'What did you do, shove it in too hard?'

'No, not me. I were asleep. It were my mother. She creeps up on me and cleans out my ears while I'm having a nap. Always has done – ever since I were a kid. I didn't know owt about it until I woke up.'

I popped back home to pick up Aileen. She had been working late into the night and had decided to ease herself gently into the new day. She was sitting at the kitchen table, eating a bowl of cornflakes with her nose up against the television screen, watching one of those daytime make-over programmes.

They were making over a suburban garden and they had to have it finished off by the time the husband came home from work at half-past five. Why they don't give themselves more time and do the job properly I shall never know.

It would be interesting to have another look at some of those *Challenge Anneka* projects, where they were

146

given twenty-four hours to build an indoor riding centre, or a classroom for disabled children. I would like to see how the wallpaper has fared after all this time, especially the one with the contemporary pattern of pale-blue chickens and the odd-looking eggs that they had to hang long before the plaster had dried properly. It would probably look rather pretty now with its bas-relief bubbles and its elegant border of green mould.

Today a team of designers were transforming the garden by applying a coat of paint to anything that had the decency to stand still long enough. They had already whipped through all the colours of the rainbow and were now working with some shades of this, that and the other that I can't ever remember having seen before.

Three of them were attacking a small fence, painting each paling a different hue, and Aileen was shouting at them, as and when the cornflakes permitted.

'For God's sake sand it down first.'

They took no notice of her, so she upped the volume.

'At least give it an undercoat. The paint'll just run off the first time it rains.' She didn't know I had joined her until I picked up the tea towel to wipe a rogue cornflake from the television screen.

'You have a look. Is that emulsion they're using?'

I had a look.

'Looks like it.'

'How silly.'

She switched it off.

'Not a patch on *Ground Force.*'

I must admit we do rather like watching *Ground Force*. It's more fun than the others and Aileen has always had a soft spot for Alan Titchmarsh, ever since she worked with him at a literary luncheon, while I tend to sit back with a glass of red wine and concentrate most of my attention on Charlie Dimmock, the blonde lady with the wonderful nipples.

The cats were out in the garden as we left the house. Thermal was deadheading the roses – he's very good at it and getting better all the time. The other cats can't understand his horticultural obsession. They are into the more traditional feline pursuits such as hunting, shooting and fishing, although I must admit I can't remember the last time they shot anything.

They are also heavily into the preservation of territorial rights. First thing in the morning Tigger likes to check all the hedges, sniffing at almost each and every leaf with the utmost dedication.

It's rather like a wine tasting. She sniffs delicately at first and then, gulping in the tell-tale evidence, she swishes the aroma around the back of her throat.

'Mmmm! Small short-hair kitten, female tabby with a slight limp in her left back leg. Passed through the hedge at around 6.37 this morning, probably on her way to do her paper round.'

Sometimes she jumps back in alarm, her eyes crossed and running with tears.

'Yuk! Denton – and he's been eating garlic again.'

But Thermal takes his deadheading just as seriously and his commitment to the cause is a lesson to us all. His interest in roses started last summer when a kamikaze wasp took a deep breath, plucked up the courage, and dive-bombed him from behind.

Thermal wasn't having that. He chased it all over the garden and then watched as it settled on the petals of a geriatric rose that had but a few short hours to live.

He moved in silently and belted both rose and wasp with a crisp right-hander. Whatever happened to the wasp we shall never know, but the rose gave a deep sigh and disintegrated immediately, its petals falling gracefully, showering Thermal until he looked like a bridesmaid at a posh society wedding.

That small moment changed his life for ever and since then he has kept a close eye on the roses. He moves through the garden tapping every one from in-experienced bud to fully grown adult. His disappoint-ment on those occasions when they merely lean back and roll with the blow is more than compensated for when the older ones collapse and rain petals down on his head.

Once he's sorted out the smaller bushes I go and fetch the kitchen steps for him. They are on castors and I push him around the garden as he tackles those that would otherwise be out of reach.

I waved the two cats goodbye, opened the car door for Aileen, then bent and lifted William out from under the back wheel. As I carried him out of harm's way and sat him on the wall he gazed back longingly over my shoulder at his unattended drain.

'We'll be gone in a minute, then you can go back.'

He seemed to understand, but as I climbed into the car Thermal came stalking out of the gate, bristling with indignation.

'We'll be back by lunchtime, then I'll get the steps out for you.'

He relaxed and forgave me.

'*Thank you.*'

'My pleasure.'

'*Have a nice time.*'

The film crew had moved down to Byram Street and taken over Neaverson's china shop, opposite the parish church. I parked the car and we walked back through a tight little band of sightseers who were having to make do with gawping at the sound engineer since it is almost impossible to see in through Neaverson's modernistic windows.

Inside they were rehearsing a rewrite of scene nine and I experienced my first dialogue cut. Since this was Penny Downie's first appearance as Aileen I had wanted to show the audience that she was blind without going over the top. No white sticks or anything like that, just Pete describing each ornament as she picks it up. At the same time he would be telling her about the strange way in which my mother had bought her house.

DERIC: So she gazumped herself by £5,000 in as many seconds.

Aileen picks up an ornament and is puzzled. She runs her hands over it.

AILEEN: Still. It could all turn out for the best in the long run, couldn't it? What's this?

DERIC: It's a frog. It's got a sort of hat on. It's just the family home gone for ever. She's been there for almost forty years, you know.

Aileen is still puzzled by the ornament.

DERIC: It's carrying a set of golf clubs and a fishing rod.

Aileen grimaces and puts it down in disgust.

Of course I knew that the props buyer was going to have a bit of trouble finding a china frog with a sort of hat on, who just happened to be carrying a set of golf clubs and a fishing rod, but I was prepared to compromise. I had already combed the gift shops of West Yorkshire and I knew exactly where I could lay my hands on a pair of youth-hostelling rabbits who were wearing khaki shorts and Doc Martens while carrying a haversack apiece and sporting a couple of stout walking sticks to assist them on their cross-country stroll. They'd be just the job.

But we cut the lines anyway. They weren't really needed, and Sita Williams was worried that the script might run a few minutes over time. The commercials are sacrosanct.

For the moment we were surplus to requirements. The china shop was already packed solid with people who were busy doing proper jobs such as lighting, directing and acting, so we popped outside and left them to it.

As we mingled with the crowd of onlookers we were joined by a couple of ladies in blue overalls who seemed very excited by the whole business, except that they had their backs to us and were staring across the road at the parish church.

'What is it, a wedding?'

One of the crew had a word with them, explaining the situation, and they listened to her with faces as blank as two sheets of A4 paper. But they thanked her anyway and when another friend joined them they were able to fill her in with the necessary details.

'Who's getting married then?'

'Simon Armitage apparently.'

'What – the poet?'

'Must be.'

'From Marsden?'

'Yes, that's the one. That's why this lot are all here.'

She gestured dismissively over her shoulder at the crew who were now beginning to wrap things up. But the women waited on, shuffling from one foot to the other while making sure their Sainsbury's carrier bags remained upright and alert. Occasionally they glanced at their watches. It wouldn't matter if they were a few minutes late for work.

'You'd have thought he'd have got married in Marsden, wouldn't you?'

'Mmmm.'

'Maybe she wouldn't have it. Put her foot down. Who is she anyway?'

'Some model, I shouldn't wonder.'

There was a communal sniff of disapproval.

'All the same, aren't they?'

I took Aileen Armitage by the arm and guided her back to the car. The women were framed in my rear-view mirror as I pulled out into the traffic, still staring across at the empty church. I just hope that Simon lives happily ever after, with his Naomi or his Kate or who-ever she is – he's a nice lad.

Women of a certain age have always proved a rich vein of material for me. After a talk I gave in Sheffield a doctor's receptionist told me the story of a rather refined old lady who had been asked to bring in a urine sample so that they could send it away for tests.

She was back later that Monday afternoon carrying a small brown-paper bag and, shielding it with her body from the others in the waiting room, she produced from it a delicate little vinegar bottle in finest mock Wedgwood, with a tiny cork stopper in the neck.

She liked things to be nice, she told the receptionist.

On the Saturday morning she was waiting outside as the surgery opened for business.

'Sorry to bother you, but do you think I could possibly have my vinegar bottle back? Only we're off on a trip to Fountains Abbey tomorrow and it's part of my picnic set.'

I've never really enjoyed a plate of fish and chips since.

Straight after lunch I set to work. I had deadlines to meet and the fading light had driven the film crew back to the studios in Leeds. I must have sat at my desk for a couple of hours or so and while I was away in another world the cats had drifted into my office and quietly spread themselves around the room.

By the time I came back to reality my shoulders ached and my legs were freezing, tucked away as they were under the desk, in the pigeon-hole between the two sets of drawers.

I unscrewed the top off my insulated jug of coffee and poured myself a cup, then lit a cigarette, swung my legs out from under the desk and dangled them in the gulf stream of hot air that flows directly between the Valor living flame and the radiator on the wall behind me.

The weirdest sight greeted my eyes. The sun had come out to play once more and I was surrounded by a herd of multi-coloured cats.

There was a red one over by the fireplace and a bright blue one lying flat on his back on the table in the window. Another red one, of a slightly more crimson hue this time, was fast asleep on that bit that sticks out from the bookcase and there was a green-and-yellow-striped tortoiseshell just below him, stretched out on the carpet.

For a moment I wondered what sort of cigarette I was smoking and decided that Dunhill must have started putting some of that funny stuff in them.

'Aileen, come and look at this.'

Which is a pretty stupid thing to yell to a woman who can't even see her hand in front of her face. She appeared from out of her study.

'What?'

'The cats. They're all sorts of colours. Thermal's gone blue.'

A look of horror passed across her face. Had he stopped breathing? Should she give him the kiss of life?

'It's the stained-glass windows, love. The cats have each picked out a different spot of sunlight and now they're all the colours of the rainbow.'

As the sun shifted its position in the sky, the cats shifted their position in the room, seeking out fresh pastures in which to soak up the warmth. Tigger moved a foot to her left and instantly turned a bright emerald green. Thermal, half in the sunshine and half out, swopped his electric blue duffle coat for a pair of tailored jogging pants in a rather fetching shade of pale lilac.

It was as though I had been transported to an *Alice in Wonderland* world where anything was possible, especially when William glared at me through a pair of deep green eyes that clashed awfully with the orange tips of his whiskers. He had looked so much better before Technicolor arrived, back in the old black and white days when cats were cats and not some sort of mobile fashion accessory.

Then Thermal shifted his position once more, this time slipping into a little pale pink number with adjustable shoulder straps and matching bootees.

I gave Aileen a running commentary on the changing scene but it was still some time before it dawned on me that we now had four cats and not just the resident three.

'Hey, Little Chap's back.'

'Is he?'

'Yes. He's the red one over there by the bit that sticks out from the bookcase.'

We went over to have a closer look at him, to see

what sort of state he was in this time and as I drew nearer all the redness drained out of him. It was a strange experience, as though the Technicolor cat had been beamed up by Scotty, and I realized that to witness the full psychedelic effect one had to view the scene from a certain angle, like sitting over there at my desk.

He was knackered as usual but as I turned him over, this way and that, he didn't appear to be any the worse for his latest expedition. Thinner, yes, but otherwise all in one piece. Odd bits of fur here and there were hanging on by a thread, but that was pretty good going for Little Chap.

Aileen was waiting anxiously for my verdict.

'Is he all right?'

I turned him over and had another good look underneath.

'Yes. He seems to be fine.'

Unconscious, but fine. William came over to give me a second opinion. He sniffed here and he sniffed there, and then he sniffed there again and that seemed to touch a nerve with Little Chap. His eyes shot wide open but it took a little time for them to warm up.

First there was a deep vacant space as though there was nobody at home and the answerphone had been switched off. Then as the wheels in his brain began to turn and the pulleys in his memory began to do whatever it is that pulleys are supposed to do, a little light began to dawn and his head began to move like the gun turret in a Sherman tank.

He saw Tigger and then he saw Thermal and then he felt William's cold nose as it closed in on him once more, just to make sure. Then he leaped to his feet and saw me kneeling above him and he threw back his head.

'*Foo-oo-oo-ood.*'

Aileen relaxed. We could rebuild him.

Chapter Twelve

I was in the front line, fielding the phone for Aileen, when Annie Ashurst rang me around half-past ten in the morning. If the name doesn't immediately ring a bell, allow me to fill you in.

Annie is that wonderful woman who romped away with the *Mastermind* title in the very last programme of the TV series, and she's a very good friend of mine.

Me. The man who not only failed each and every examination he ever took in his life, but who also once scored a perfect zero in woodwork at the Manor Secondary School in Chesterfield. It's a record that stands to this day.

Annie is a feisty, multi-talented lady – the breadth of her knowledge is mind-bending. She's also a cricket fanatic and under the pseudonym of Sara Craven she writes best-selling romances for Mills and Boon, always to the accompaniment of a roof-lifting barrage of hard rock music.

She also is the proud possessor of a tongue so cutting that it could probably pass a woodwork examination all on its own, no problem.

You don't mess with Annie, but as a friend she is

truly loyal and at times extremely useful. If you are ever stuck for an answer in the middle of a family quiz, what better than to sneak out into the hall, pick up the phone, and have a one-to-one with the winner of the *Mastermind* title? Slightly dishonest, I agree, but it works for me.

She wanted to talk to Aileen but it really wasn't on just then. That's why I was fielding the phone.

'Can she ring you back, Annie? Only she's talking to her computer at the moment.'

Annie quite understood.

'I often talk to mine. I say, you stupid wanker, what the bloody hell do you think you're playing at?'

Life has been much easier for Aileen since she dispensed with the keyboard and began to dictate straight into the computer. They make quite a team, the two of them. They spend hours together, chatting away happily, but if someone happens to barge in on her unannounced or the phone suddenly rings, then the computer goes into a mad panic and a whole stream of gibberish appears on the screen.

She has to shut it down in an orderly manner. She leans forward and breathes into the microphone.

'Go to sleep.'

The computer doesn't argue. It's probably glad of the break and I like to think that somewhere deep inside this highly intelligent lump of machinery, a tiny piece of software has a good long stretch and then manages to grab a quick five minutes while the going's good.

When she's ready to start work again Aileen leans forward once more.

'Wake up.'

Sometimes the computer takes a little time to obey

the command, but before long the two of them are back on the same wavelength.

'Sorry about that, Aileen. I was on the toilet. Just downloading a few megabytes. Now then, what can I do for you?'

So I answer the door and look after the phone for her and most days I'm up and down like a jackrabbit. Friends want to know why I don't simply leave the answerphone on and deal with the calls later, but I can't do that.

There was a time, long ago, when I wanted to hide behind the settee whenever the phone burst into life. It was bound to be either the Gas or the Electricity Board threatening to send in the heavies if I didn't cough up immediately – either that or the Midland Bank asking very politely if I would be kind enough to pop in for a quiet word.

But things have changed since then and nowadays, apart from the odd special offer from a double-glazing firm who just happen to be in my area, the news is generally good, ranging from the extremely pleasant to the downright exciting.

So the moment I hear the answerphone begin to clear its throat I'm off down two flights of stairs to listen in and find out who's on the other end, and then since I'm down there anyway I might as well take over and have a word with them.

My granddaughter Katie rang ten minutes after Annie to tell me about her trip to London Zoo. Katie is seven years old going on thirty-five.

'I was very disappointed in the giraffes.'

She had especially wanted to see the giraffes.

'They weren't as tall as I expected.'

I heard her mother's voice in the background. It was a voice under pressure, a voice that was trying to keep an eye on things while at the same time pulling a load of wet clothes out of the washing machine.

'That's because they were a long way away, Katie.'

'They were smaller than the gorilla.'

The voice butted in once more.

'Because they were a long way away.'

'The gorilla was very nice.'

I managed to get a word in.

'You liked the gorilla, did you?'

That's the sort of stupid remark grandfathers make to their offspring once removed. Of course she liked the gorilla – she'd just told me. I don't get enough practice at this sort of thing.

'Yes, he smiled a lot, but the giraffes were very small.'

Sally's voice passed by on the way to the tumble dryer. It had gone up a couple of notches on the Beaufort scale.

'Because they were over the other side of the field. You tell her, Dad.'

Stuff that. She's their kid. Grandfathers are there to be loved, not to give lectures.

'What else did you see?'

She gave me a quick rundown on all the other animals and then went through the menu in the coffee shop, item by item.

'So you had a good time?'

'Yes. Apart from the giraffes.'

The next call was from Alan Bell, the director of *Lost for Words*.

'Are you thinking of coming over today?'

I hadn't. The day before I had spent a full eight hours

hanging around a garden centre, watching the longest scene in the play wither before my eyes.

Thora was supposed to wander along a rack stacked with packets of rose fertilizer, picking up each identical packet, reading the identical instructions on the back of each packet as though she were seeing them for the first time, which in effect she was, with her befuddled mind.

She would then move on to a shelf stacked with identical packets of slug pellets and do exactly the same. I was trying to show how this fragile mind of hers had deteriorated, that she remembered very little from one moment to the next.

But during the early script conferences it had been suggested that I might make more of this and at the time it had seemed rather a good idea. Thora, on seeing the packets of slug pellets, each decorated with a large picture of a big black slug, would be frightened and recoil, being reminded of the slugs she imagined were invading her house and making her life a misery.

'Little devils.'

Pete would rush over and comfort her, explaining that the packets didn't really contain slugs, but the poison to kill them, and this would give her an idea. 'Poison,' she would mutter thoughtfully as Pete led her away.

But it didn't work. This wasn't the way it had really happened. Her mind at that time wouldn't have stretched to such an idea and it detracted from the main point of the scene.

Added to that, the packets of slug pellets seemed to take over the whole set. They had been brilliantly concocted out of boxes of cornflakes, disguised and decorated with a huge black slug who sneered out at the world, daring anyone to mess with him.

'Come on, punk – make my day.'

They had a cartoon quality about them and although

they had been a considerable investment in time and ingenuity, they just weren't right.

The extra business also denied Thora the space to do what she does best. As I wrote the scene I had closed my eyes and watched her doing it over and over in my head and I knew she would be wonderful. With just a twitch of her nose and a raised eyebrow she would examine each packet closely before putting it back and reaching out for another. It's impossible for Thora to be boring and the repetition would establish how far her understanding had deteriorated.

But the new business had intruded, allowing time for her to examine only a couple of packets, and the point was missed. From that moment on nothing seemed to work. My lines came out forced and wooden and I just wanted to run away and hide.

So I had decided to give it a miss today, but Alan thought differently.

'We're shooting the party scene in your mother's old house. Be handy if you were there.'

Andrew Sanderson had recreated my mother's lounge in the studios at Leeds and I was looking forward to seeing it. He and Josh Dynevor, the location manager, hadn't been able to get into her first house in Chesterfield, so they'd had to make do with peeping in through the windows and then let their imagination tell them how the room might have appeared some twenty years earlier.

And they had it just about right. It was uncanny. The brick fireplace, the french windows and the general layout of the room they would have seen, but the bric-à-brac, the furnishings and the general feel of the house were spot on. I half expected my mother to put her head round the kitchen door.

*　　*　　*

I joined a group of extras who were watching Thora run through a scene with Anne Reid and Keith Clifford. Between takes the conversation around me always seemed to come back to who the extras had worked with in the past and what they had lined up in the near future.

'Of course I've worked with Thora before. On *Last of the Summer Wine.*'

'Yes, I've done a couple of those and I've got an *Emmerdale* coming up shortly.'

Peak Practice, Heart of the Matter and *Heartbeat* were all tossed around in a cavalier show of one-upmanship. *Coronation Street* and *Brookside* zipped in and out of the conversation until I felt I had been beamed down into some sort of Yorkshire Hollywood.

One of the extras had held the door open for Kevin in the Rover's Return and apparently the whole scene revolved about this seemingly innocent action. Maybe he was right. Kevin wouldn't have been able to come in if he hadn't.

Another of them chipped in with an *Inspector Morse* appearance and that shut everybody up for a while. In between bouts of looking smug he quietly sang to himself, snatches of Nat King Cole's 'Let There Be Love'.

' "Laurel and Hardy / *dum dum* / Sparkling champagne." '

I knew there was something wrong with that somewhere but I couldn't think what it was and I worried about it all afternoon.

A kindly soul tried to include me in the conversation.

'You done anything lately?'

'Not a lot.'

'It seems to come in runs, doesn't it?'

'Yes.'

He picked up a script from a nearby table.

'Who's the writer? Not Alan Bennett, is it?'

There was a small snort from down the line.

'Nah.'

The man with the script rifled back through the sheets of A4 until he came across the title page.

'Deric Longden.'

The snorter snorted once more.

'Never heard of him.'

My friend came to my rescue.

'Probably some kid. They've got a good cast for him, though. Worth keeping an eye on.'

I promised I would do just that and went off to the toilet where I twirled around twice like Superman and immediately changed back into the writer.

We broke for lunch and everyone trooped off to the canteen, with the exception of Dame Thora. She wasn't at all well, and the thought of being hauled about in her wheelchair once more was too much for her, so she had her lunch brought to her on the set. It consisted of three cream buns which served as her starter, main course and pudding. I grabbed a cup of coffee, pulled up a foot-stool, and kept her company.

We talked about how, some three years ago in the Huddersfield Hotel, we had sat down over dinner with Aileen and discussed how we were going to adapt the book for television. During the intervening years several people who had a good track record in the medium, been there and done that and knew better than I did, had told me that it wouldn't work.

'Not enough story. Too little action.'

But I had Thora, and I knew we could make it work. Ever since she played my mother in *Wide-Eyed and Legless* I was sure that, with Thora's interpretation of

163

my mother's generous and eccentric behaviour, we could turn it into a winner.

We didn't need car crashes, multiple murders or lurid rape scenes. It's the small moments in life that stick in the memory. People can come through a war and put it all behind them, but they never forget a hurt inflicted when they were nine years old and vulnerable as hell.

What I did need, however, was a structure, and that was a long time in coming. It had to be tighter than the book, and it wasn't until eighteen months later, when I decided upon a flashback through a series of old photographs, that the play began to take shape.

Those photographs were on the mantelpiece behind me now as I sat talking with Thora. There was me in my little white bootees and my little white angora coat and bonnet, with my rosy pink cheeks artificially coloured in and my lips touched up to perfection with a bright red lipstick by Rimmel. I have often thought that I reached my peak on the day that photograph was taken and it's been downhill ever since.

Then there was my mother as a beautiful young woman on a day out in Blackpool, with the tower in the background, wearing a coat that long since went out of fashion and then came back in again quite recently.

Nuzzling up to this was a photograph of Thora taken just a few days before, with her looking for all the world the spitting image of my mother in her later years.

Slotted in between these three were several photographs of Pete as a small boy, first in short trousers and then as a teenager in football boots, charting the progress of my life from the little white bootees to the photograph of my wedding to Aileen, as posed professionally by Pete Postlethwaite and Penny Downie. You could hardly see the join.

*   *   *

Thora had thought it over and decided to save the cream bun with the chocolate icing for her pudding – it seemed to be the right thing to do. You can't go having a cream bun covered in chocolate as a main course.

I sipped my coffee and listened to her. That's the way a conversation with Thora usually goes. At first there is a certain ebb and flow and then the duologue becomes a monologue and I never mind a bit. She's far more interesting than I am and I could listen to her for hours, and often have.

As she talked I began to take in the room about us. The sideboard just like my mother's, the battered but comfortable settee, the blue and white cups and saucers laid out on the table. I knew without looking that if I turned them upside down the word *Empire* would be stamped underneath.

'*It's a very good make is Empire. You want to have those valued after I'm gone.*'

A sewing box – hardly used. On the dresser a row of suspicious-looking Toby jugs all lined up, as though for an identity parade. A tea trolley fashioned out of a metal so shiny bright that it was enough to give the brass trivet an inferiority complex.

As Thora talked of her early days in show business my mind went back with her, at least part of the way, to the time when I was a little lad sitting at my mother's feet in this very room, listening to her read my father's letters from Louth in Lincolnshire where he was stationed in the Fire Service.

'*He says he loves you very much.*'

He probably did. He just had a funny way of showing it.

It was the weirdest feeling. Never mind that the set had an open end from where an off-duty camera stared down gloomily at our feet, or that without the saving grace of special lighting the trees and houses through the French windows were obviously painted on to a vast backcloth.

For a short while it was all very real, until one by one and two by two the cast and crew began to drift back on to the set, the extras sticking together in a tight little bunch.

'Did I tell you about when I was in *Wokenwell*?'

Pete Postlethwaite was fed up to the teeth. He had cut short his lunch break to give an interview to a couple of journalists up from London for the day. He had wanted to talk about the play and they had been asking him about the house where he'd been born in Warrington.

'Did it have an outside toilet?'

'What the hell's that got to do with anything?'

This unfortunately is the lot of any actor who happens to have been born up here in the north. Did your dad work down the pit and did he keep pigeons?

'No. He was a barrister.'

'He'd have had a whippet though, wouldn't he?'

Pete is a star and a good man to have around. Steven Spielberg says that without doubt he is one of the four best character actors in the world and we were lucky to have been able to grab him for the whole of one of those rare months when he wasn't hard at work in the United States.

His concentration is total, but he always has time for the younger members of the cast and loves nothing better than a pint with the crew in the nearest pub.

While we were filming I had to pop over to Rochdale to talk at a conference of hospital broadcasters and in the bar beforehand I had several drinks with a total stranger who worked as a stunt co-ordinator in the movies.

Now coming across a big-time stunt co-ordinator in Rochdale is amazing in itself, but we also found that we had Pete in common. This man had spent a week with him, driving around in a small van on location in Africa. He thought Pete was the bee's knees and talked of little else for the best part of an hour, but even Mr Postlethwaite was upstaged when Henry arrived on the set.

Some actors prefer to drift in quietly, unannounced, but Henry was the master of the grand entrance. He strode proudly through the spaghetti mass of wires and cables as though he were on his way up to collect his Oscar, back straight as a ramrod, his red lead and collar marking him out as the sort of cat who could always be relied upon to turn in a sound performance.

His handler slipped him off the leash and parked him on the back of my mother's settee. He took in the scene around him as Allan Pyrah and Dave Carey tried out a few dummy shots with the camera.

'*Bloody amateurs.*'

I could imagine him sitting up late into the night, working on his moves with the script laid out in front of him.

'*Now what is my motivation when Dame Thora drops me four feet on to a solid concrete step?*'

His handler whispered into his ear.

'Sit.'

And so he sat and then never moved a muscle for the next fifteen minutes. At drama school he had received a special commendation for the quality of his sitting and it was a skill that had come in very handy throughout his short career.

You get involved in a lot of sitting when you are playing the part of a cat. But he hoped that future roles might stretch him even further so that eventually he could introduce his famous dead mouse routine or maybe do that fancy dribbling thing with the ping-pong ball. He was also planning to take fencing lessons.

I had been very careful when writing the cat into the action. Cats can't act – end of story. But then, of course, that was before I met Henry, so how was I to know?

We did need a cat. My mother could talk to it, letting the audience in on secrets that she would never tell me. There were also several funny bits and pieces that I didn't want to lose.

My mother regularly washed Whisky in the kitchen. She would lather him up in one sink and then rinse him off in the other.

'This double drainer's been a blessing.'

Whether the cat thought it a blessing or not I shall never know, but I remember he always looked down-right miserable as she stood him on the draining board and towelled him down before fluffing him up with the hair dryer. Every now and then, for a special treat, she used to hoover him.

I knew we couldn't expect a stand-in cat to put up with all that sort of nonsense, it would run a mile, so I had written the scene so that Henry would be able to do just that.

Scene 11. Interior of Mother's old house – kitchen – day.

Deric's mother is about to wash the cat in the kitchen sink. It's full of foaming liquid. She wears rubber gloves, one yellow, the other pink, and she has the cat trapped on the draining board.

MOTHER: It's no good grumbling. If you made a better job of it yourself there'd be no need for this.

The doorbell rings and, as she turns towards the sound, the cat makes a break for it.

MOTHER: Whisky – come here. Oh damn it.

Pulling off the rubber gloves as she goes, she exits towards the kitchen door.

MOTHER: Take me ages to catch him again.

Cut to hallway.

We had shot the scene earlier in the week but of course the RSPCA would have had our guts for garters if we had plunged Henry head first into the sink, so we'd stuck him on the draining board and let Thora have her wicked way with him.

She soaked him and lathered him, rubbing bubbles into his important little places, but would he jump off? Would he hell. He loved every minute of it.

'I think you've missed a bit, Thora. Just under my armpit, left front.'

Take after take we tried again. Thora was just about as wet as the cat.

'Do my tail again, Thora. Run it through your fingers. Slowly. There, that's right. Oh God, that's wonderful.'

In the end Alan Bell had to sit Henry on a tea towel that hung over the edge of the draining board. He placed a man strategically, down by the side of the sink unit, and then as Thora began to lather the cat once more the man yanked the tea towel and Henry, wondering why his feet were suddenly disappearing from underneath him, finally called it a day and leaped to the floor.

If ever I have the opportunity to work with Henry again I shall write him a scene where he has his split ends seen to and his ears pierced.

*   *   *

Today, however, it was his sitting skills that were called for. With a huge red bow slung around his neck he was required to sit on a pouffe for as long as it took my mother to show a bevy of would-be buyers around her house.

He must have learned a lot sitting there. It was like a masterclass. Anne Reid and Keith Clifford were wonderful, and when the widower from North Wingfield, played by Eddie Caswell, walked on to the set I could hardly believe my eyes. He was a dead ringer for the bloke who came to look round the house all those years ago.

Bemused by all the bustle and further embarrassed by the scrutiny of all the women in the room, he hesitates and then apologizes.

WIDOWER: I seem to have picked the wrong time.
MOTHER: Not at all. No. Is your mother not with you?
WIDOWER: No. (*Beat*) She's got her leg up again.
MOTHER: You don't have to tell me about legs. I've got one myself.

Henry sat perfectly still on his pouffe and took it all in, making mental notes of Thora's immaculate timing. He could build on that in a few minutes when it came to his big moment.

And he did. As Pete entered and then moved towards the settee, Henry shot off his pouffe like the born athlete he undoubtedly is, bounded across the carpet, leaped up on to the settee and then scooted over the back and out of the room.

Another shot in the can, another day's work well done. He called for his driver and without a backward glance departed from the set.

'*Probably pop in tomorrow to have a look at the rushes.*'

*   *   *

I smiled all the way home. Alan Bell and his team had lifted the scene straight from the page and breathed life into it. Everything had gone like clockwork and the previous day's shoot in the garden centre, with the help of a little early editing and the disappearance of the slug pellets, didn't look so bad after all. Now if I could only get this damn tune out of my head, all would be right with the world.

' "Laurel and Hardy / *dum dum* / Sparkling champagne." '

I must have sung that line a hundred times between Leeds and Huddersfield. I knew Laurel and Hardy had no business being in there, but no matter how I tried I couldn't come up with the original words.

I messed around with a varied combination of cuckoos, larks and doves but I still hadn't worked it out by the time I arrived home.

Aileen had laid the table and opened a bottle of white wine. She was already two glasses ahead of me.

'I thought it was red.'

It didn't matter as it happened. I had planned to cook a couple of steaks but they were still buried deep in the freezer. Aileen took the news philosophically, as you do when you've already had a couple of glasses of white wine.

'Never mind. Let's have some pasta – and there's that leftover chilli con carne in the fridge.'

I kissed the top of her head. That was it!

' "Chilli con carne/*dum dum*/Sparkling champagne." '

Over dinner I told her how clever she was and as always she wholeheartedly agreed with me. Then I told her all about having lunch with Thora and about the extras and about Henry the cat and how, with just another little tweak here and there, we could rescue the scene in the garden centre and she beamed and was ever so pleased for me.

Some days you just can't go wrong, can you?

Chapter Thirteen

I sometimes worry about myself. There are times when I wonder whether I might be losing it. My mind, I mean.

I had made an overnight trip down to Bournemouth where I spoke to some very nice people in the Pavilion, but then as I prepared to point the car north for the long journey home I found that the automatic gears had gone on strike and had decided to stay put in P for parking.

Jiggling about didn't do much good and neither did a bout of strenuous yanking and so, having worked my way through my extensive knowledge of all things mechanical, with special reference to automatic gears, I resorted to switching the engine on and off several times and suddenly there was a click and we were back in business once more.

On the way home I stopped off at a Little Chef for a quick cup of coffee, a free newspaper and to experience the unalloyed pleasure of hearing the one-sided conversations of people nattering away on their mobile phones.

They were all company men and women, two of them sitting at the same table, each ignoring the other, reporting their whereabouts to some suit at headquarters.

'I'm in his outer office now. Hope to get in to see him before lunchtime.'

As I sipped my coffee – the Little Chef's coffee is going downhill, by the way, they'd even managed to burn the water this time – as I sat there and sipped and winced and looked around me, I wondered if those brandishing their mobile phones realized that in most cases they are merely a modern refinement of that row of bells in the big house, the ones that used to be slung high above the door in the servants' quarters.

'We want you. Now.'

It was fun to try to work out the status of each of these mobile phone-a-philes. The smug little man bawling out instructions from behind the potted plant was bound be the Butler and there was the Housekeeper over there, her eyebrows dancing with frustration as she listened to a string of miserable excuses trotted out by one of her minions on the other end.

We didn't seem to have the Cook with us, as far as I could see, but the Downstairs Maid had obviously made a pig's ear of the dusting and she was getting a right telling off. I don't think she'd said a word in the past ten minutes.

Over in the corner a young man, who just had to be the Boots, was squirming in his plastic seat, his polyester suit shiny with embarrassment as its owner was told for the umpteenth time to pull his finger out.

I was feeling a right little smart-arse as I climbed in the car and switched on the ignition, but that lovely glow of self-assurance faded somewhat over the next twenty minutes as I sat there and jiggled and yanked and switched the engine on and off.

My imaginary domestic staff filed out of the Little Chef one by one and then roared off out of the car park in their Escorts and Mondeos with not a care in the world. I was right about the Butler by the way – he had a black Lexus with a personalized number plate.

All of which didn't help me one jot, and I was just about to call the AA when my foot accidentally brushed against the brake pedal and there was a little click and it was all systems go once more.

The next morning I decided I had better get my gears sorted out. For the time being a gentle tap on the brake pedal would bring them into play but it was obviously only a temporary measure and things were bound to go from bad to worse.

The lovely Sharon was behind her desk and Mark the mechanic came out to have a word with me. I sank into the deep leather chair and told him all about the trouble I'd had in Bournemouth and at the Little Chef.

'. . . but I've found if I tap the brake pedal it seems to work.'

Mark waited patiently for me to carry on but there wasn't any more to say.

'That's it really.'

He settled his right shoulder against the nearest wall and took a deep breath and I saw in his eyes a look that I have seen quite often over the years. It's known as the 'we've got a right one here' sort of look and I would recognize it a mile off.

'How long did you have your previous Jaguar?'

'Three years.'

'And how long have you had this one?'

'Three months.'

He took a deep breath.

'And in all that time you never realized that you have to press the brake pedal to release the gears?'

That's when I first realized I must be losing it.

'I can't have.'

'You must have.'

He took pity on me.

'Give me the keys and I'll go and have a look at it.'

I handed them over, squirming in my leather chair. I smiled at Sharon.

'You won't tell anybody, will you.'

'Yes, of course I will.'

Mark returned a few minutes later, waving my dipstick in the air as though he were about to conduct the Huddersfield Choral Society.

'When did you last put any oil in?'

Now I had him there.

'Yesterday afternoon. At a Shell station just outside Oxford.'

I bet not many of his customers can pinpoint their movements quite as accurately as that. I thought he would be impressed.

'Pity you didn't think to screw the cap back on the oil tank.'

He took me to have a look at my car. My lovely 4.2 engine was a disaster area. It reminded me of when the *Amoco Cadiz* split in half and 50,000 tons of crude oil made straight for the beaches of Brittany. There was oil everywhere, smothering the engine and the under-side of the bonnet.

'It must be all over your garage floor.'

'I didn't see any – I reverse out.'

Mark stuck his hand down by the radiator and I half expected him to come up with a mucky-looking seagull that was going to sue me for every penny I'd got. Instead he produced my missing oil cap.

'That's something anyway.'

He spent ages steam-cleaning the engine and blowing

it dry, then he dried the spark plugs on a cloth and put them back. The engine purred into life.

'You've been lucky.'

I didn't really want to be that lucky ever again. I don't think I have ever felt such a prat in my life – well I have, but we won't go into that at the moment.

On the way out I had another chat with Sharon.

'You won't really tell anybody, will you?'

'No, of course not.'

So the whole episode remains a close secret between the three of us, Sharon and Mark and me – plus half the population of Huddersfield. It's nice when you know you can trust people.

At least I had the car back in time to make a start on my list. As a result of the filming we were getting a little behind with the nuts and bolts of life, those small insignificant jobs that don't matter at all until you string half a dozen of them together and find that life doesn't run so smoothly any more.

I called in and signed something at the accountant's. I have no idea what it was, but Roger Armitage had told me to call in and sign it – so I did.

He also told me that he'd been at a conference over the weekend and when they returned from lunch they discovered that someone had gone and stolen three laptop computers from the meeting room.

As they left to go home that night they found that they had also had three cars stolen from outside the hotel. One of his colleagues had a solution.

'They want their hands chopping off.'

Another colleague chipped in.

'It doesn't work.'

'How do you mean?'

'My wife works for the Social Security. She had to

refuse benefit to a man with no arms – so he head-butted her.'

I left the car where it was and walked the fifty yards across to Sainsbury's. It's not something I would normally do but they say exercise is good for you and I thought I would give it a try.

There were two dogs tied up outside. One of them was a big black mongrel and the other a posh-looking poodle with a pedigree as long as your arm.

The poodle was attached to the railings by an exquisitely plaited lead that would have had Gucci stamped all over it had their designer decided to take a sideways step into dog accessories.

The hair was definitely by Vidal Sassoon and you have to admit that he does give a damn good cut, no matter what his own hair looks like. This dog would have been quite at home on the catwalks of London, Paris or Milan, but he did look a bit daft tied up to the railings outside the Huddersfield branch of Sainsbury's.

The mongrel, however, had been secured to the railings by a tatty piece of string that had been called upon to tackle one job too many. I say secured – the piece of string had been draped on the floor quite near the railings and wasn't attached to anything other than thin air. But the dog didn't know that, he was too busy wagging his tail and rolling his eyes at all who passed him by, collecting pats on the head until one feared that he might suffer brain damage.

I see him around town quite a lot, sometimes in the company of a small Irishman but more often than not out walking on his own. I assumed he must be with the Irishman today – he was hardly likely to have tied himself up to the railings, however loosely.

He's a good dog and he knows his way around, especially when it comes to traffic lights. He stops at the pavement edge and looks first left and then right and then left again. Then he marches straight across the road whether there's anything coming or not. At least you know where you are with him.

We had a few words and a lick and a pat. He did the licking and I did the patting. I wiped my damp hand on his coat, which was what had brought me over to have a look at them in the first place.

While the pedigree poodle was all dressed up like a dog's dinner, it was the mongrel who was wearing the brand new tartan jacket with the shiny plastic straps and the two little sleeves that stretched down over his haunches as far as his knees.

There's democracy for you. However lowly born, you can still reach for the stars, even if they do turn out to be tartan with plastic straps.

'You look very smart.'

'*Thank you.*'

I can usually nip round Sainsbury's in a matter of minutes, but they'd had a refit while I was away and I couldn't find a damn thing. Neither could anyone else. We should have been roped together and taken on a guided tour.

It took me ages to find the small Atlantic prawns and the coley steaks. They were where the white wine used to be but at least they were on offer, and so I bought six packets of each.

Fortunately the tins of tuna were where the mince used to be and the mince was where the tuna used to be, so that worked out all right. An assistant filling shelves tried to point me towards the cat food but couldn't think for the life of her where it might be, so we teamed up and spent a very pleasant half hour in each other's company. She's married but he works away a lot, so who knows where it might lead?

We chatted for a while longer as she tidied up the Kitty Treats and then we each went our separate ways, she clutching an empty cardboard box to her heaving bosom and me coquettishly swinging a hundredweight and a half of Sainsbury's own brand cat litter. And they say romance is dead.

I don't bother buying cat food any more. Well, I do – it's just that nowadays it seems to consist of small Atlantic prawns, coley steaks, mince and small tins of tuna in brine.

I am beginning to think I spoil my cats. When they first move in they will mop up anything I put in front of them and I am able to clear out all those tins of cat food that have worked their way to the back of the cupboard over the past few months, the ones that had the long-term residents turning up their collective nose.

'I don't think so – do you?'

'Wouldn't touch it with a bargepole myself.'

Even Little Chap is becoming more sophisticated. When he first arrived he would plunge his head deep into a saucer of mixed leftovers and emerge looking grateful. But then I was stupid enough to give him a tin of Sainsbury's tuna in brine and ever since then he has stalked upstairs first thing in the morning to discuss the day's menu with me in my office.

'Ah. Just the man I was looking for.'

In a few short months he has become the Ainsley Harriott of the cat world and it's driving me mad.

'I thought perhaps a chicken leg with a side salad. And do we have any feta cheese by any chance?'

The trouble is that I am already the proud owner of a

Persil-white Keith Floyd and a tortoiseshell Delia Smith and I can't be doing with any more.

Thankfully, William is still going through his Ryan Giggs period at the moment and is no trouble whatsoever. He dribbles a lot but that's about it.

Every now and then I put my foot down. I open a couple of anonymous tins and plant the contents on the kitchen floor.

'There you are. It's either that or nothing.'

The trouble is it's usually nothing. They sit in a line, a good foot away from the dish, not even deigning to look in the right direction. I can pick them up and move them a foot nearer the saucer and yet when I let go of them they are still sitting where they were originally, a good twelve inches away. I don't know how they do it.

I have tried leaving it there all day, until it looks totally inedible. But it's no good. I have never been a leader of men and as far as my cats are concerned I am merely a private in their personal Catering Corps.

On the way home I called in at the bank to sign something they wanted me to sign and then popped in to the solicitor's to sign something else. Next it was up to see Jayne, my dentist. Apparently one has to re-register every fifteen months nowadays, and I was sitting in the waiting area, catching up on Maureen Lipman's column in *Good Housekeeping*, while an elderly couple decided on which day to make an appointment for a check-up.

'We'll be at your mother's on Wednesday.'

'Thursday then.'

'York Races. What's wrong with Tuesday?'

'Oklahoma.'

'Oh aye.'

I was just thinking that they were going to have a hell of a job to get back from Oklahoma in time for her mother's on Wednesday when the man opposite me put aside his copy of *Woman and Home* and came over and sat down beside me.

'You write about your mother. Don't you?'

'I have done, yes.'

'Well, you could be writing about mine.'

He went on to tell me that his mother was always complaining about her false teeth. She had a rough bit sticking up on her top plate.

'I call in and see if she's all right every lunchtime. We have cold meat and pickles and just recently she's gone on and on about her teeth. In the end I'd just about had enough. I said I didn't want to hear any more about her blessed teeth. I told her to pop up here to the dentist's. I told her they'd have it sorted out for her in five minutes flat. But she never did.'

'What happened?'

'Well, yesterday she never mentioned them at all and so as I was leaving I asked her if she'd been up to the dentist.'

'And?'

'She said no, she hadn't. She said she'd done 'em herself on the front step.'

As I arrived home I took a good long look at the front step. Solid York stone. One hundred years old and curved at the top edge. Just the right shape for sorting out a bolshie top set.

Then I had a good look at Thermal. Aileen was worried about him.

'He doesn't seem too well.'

He hadn't bothered with his breakfast that morning. He'd decided to have a lie-in and I had taken him up a saucer of tuna just before I left.

'I'll have it later if you don't mind.'

'You all right?'

Roughly translated his symptoms seemed to suggest a cross between irritable bowel syndrome and morning sickness. But then he does put it on a bit.

'We'd better take you to the vet then.'

He didn't think so. Apparently what he needed was the top off the milk and just a smidgen of that salmon pâté Aileen and I had had for supper the night before. His mother used to swear by it.

I had left him dozing in front of the fire, but if he had managed to keep it up until now then perhaps he ought to see the vet.

There were two other cats there when we arrived at the surgery, both of them tucked up behind the bars of their portable cat baskets. An enormous Alsatian sat by the side of a little old lady who could have passed for either its owner or its lunch.

Over by the fireplace there sprawled a small round dog who seemed to have been put together by a committee, and something even more compact rustled inside a flat cardboard box that shook ominously on the knee of a teenager who wore a purple anorak and a vacant expression.

I couldn't think what he could possibly have in a box so square and flat. Perhaps it was some sort of snake, all curled up like a Danish pastry. I shuddered at the thought and Thermal dug his claws into the back of my neck and held on for dear life.

He won't have anything to do with a cat basket. He lay wrapped around my shoulders, his hot breath riffling my left ear while one of his back legs poked into the one on the right-hand side. I leaned forward a little and shuffled him up a notch.

'Thank you very much.'

'My pleasure.'

He hadn't wanted to come and I still wasn't too sure it was necessary. Aileen said he had slumped in front of the fire all day, just taking the odd trip over to his litter tray and back again whenever the urge came upon him. But since that was all he ever did during the first few months of the year she wasn't too worried about him. It wasn't until he politely declined the offer of a prawn-cocktail crisp that she was sure something was amiss.

He has been known to lie and cheat for a prawn-cocktail crisp. I wouldn't put it past him to maim and kill. And so here we were, taking our turn in the waiting room.

I had begun to suspect he had a temperature and if he hadn't, then I had. It can get awfully hot when you have a cat wrapped round the back of your neck. He whispered in my ear.

'She won't use that glass thingy, will she?'

'She might have to.'

'You won't look, will you?'

'Of course not.'

He gets most embarrassed when they take his temperature. Sitting there with a thermometer sticking out from under your tongue is one thing, having it sticking out from under your tail is another matter altogether.

The Alsatian whined piteously and the smaller dog looked across with undisguised contempt.

'Wish he wouldn't do that. Not with all these cats around. Lets us down, it does.'

The young man in the anorak was in and out of the consulting room in a flash. He still had the vacant expression but he had left his box behind with the vet and I wondered what she would be able to do for a sick snake. I wouldn't even know where to stick the thermometer.

The nurse consulted her card index and called in the next patient.

'Major Bowden.'

I waited for the Alsatian to make a move but it was the smaller dog who rose to his feet. He marched in, not waiting for his owner, back straight and head held high. All that army training, I suppose.

Thermal and I were the last to be called and the vet gave him a thorough going over.

'*Don't look.*'

'I won't.'

She gave him an injection and he was very brave. Then she felt him all over and he enjoyed that. She's known him since he was a kitten and they get on very well.

'Keep an eye on him, but I don't think there's much wrong.'

I was waiting for Thermal to get dressed when a fully grown rabbit burst into the consulting room, from the private office round the back. He did an about-turn when he saw us, skidded on the lino, and his feet went from under him. Then he crashed into the skirting board and I bent down and picked him up while he was still stunned.

'Perhaps he was frightened by the snake.'

The vet looked bemused.

'The one in the box.'

Thermal didn't talk to me all the way home. I think he was ashamed of me. But how was I to know that the vet had been out in the country all day? How was I to know that she hadn't had time to eat? How was I to know she'd ordered a pizza?

'You won't tell Aileen, will you?'

But Thermal just licked his sore bum and snorted. And after all I've done for him.

Chapter Fourteen

The next day I drove over to Horsforth and once there began looking for St Joseph's Residential Home. Earlier in the week, while the crew were filming in Seacroft Hospital, I'd had the devil's own job finding out where they were.

I know the outskirts of Leeds like the back of someone else's hand and I went round and round in circles before I eventually worked out what the temporary signs were all about.

When Yorkshire Television are filming *Heart of the Matter* they hang discreet little signs here and there, on lampposts and telegraph poles, each bearing the single word *Heart* and a small stumpy arrow. That way the caterers, the crew and the cast can find their way to that day's location.

I didn't know about this at the time and although I saw lots of yellow signs with the word *Lost* emblazoned upon them I didn't take any notice – they just seemed to be telling me what I knew already – and by the time I arrived at the Seacroft Hospital I was just about ready to book myself into the psychiatric ward. On the way home I pinched one of the *Lost* signs and it now has pride of place on my bookshelf. It seems to sum up so much of my life.

St Joseph's was an enormous old house set in its own grounds, and standing in its car park was the usual fleet of enormous television vans, pulled up alongside the caterers who had been busy serving breakfast since six-forty-five.

I sat in the car and examined the call sheet for the day. From the outside the home looked more than capable of accommodating the entire aged population of a small to medium-sized town, Harrogate, for instance. But we were going to have to make it look fully occupied with just three extras. The call sheet specified two elderly lady residents and one elderly man. They were going to have to nip about a bit.

In one stark line the call sheet also announced the acting debut of a fresh and youthful new talent.

Kitten at unit base – 1200 hours.

I imagined this small ginger kitten twisting and turning in his sleep last night, forever glancing at his alarm clock.

'Please, God, don't let me sleep in.'

His first job would be to walk in through an open door and his second, in a later scene, to jump off the bed and walk out again. He'd probably been practising for weeks and would be very nervous. This sort of chance doesn't come along all that often.

'Rolf Harris might be watching.'

I just hoped he didn't catch a glimpse of the call sheet. While the elderly ladies and the elderly man were listed as extras, they had the kitten listed under props.

After a nourishing bacon sandwich and a decent cup of coffee I went into the home and found Thora and Pete busily rehearsing a scene with Noreen Kershaw and our two elderly lady residents.

Although it was still early, with a definite chill in the air, Thora and Pete had already been out filming an earlier scene in which my mother suddenly sees the nursing home through the car windscreen.

They are supposed to be driving home from the garden centre. My mother is downcast, with no life in her face, and Pete is attempting to cheer her up. Suddenly she sees a large house on the other side of the road. It's the one she's been trying to tell him about ever since the stroke robbed her of any recognizable form of language.

MOTHER: Spongo.

Deric's eye follows the line of her finger. We see a sign: Springbank Nursing Home.

DERIC: That's Spongo!

A car pips them and Deric sets off again. His mother turns to him.

MOTHER: Spongo.

She stares down lifelessly at the dashboard.

MOTHER: Ready. So ready.

In the finished product the scene brought tears to the eyes, especially to mine. And yet it was filmed at just after seven o'clock on a cold spring morning with the car window rolled right down, and by a camera mounted on a steel frame strapped to the outside of the vehicle.

At that time in the morning the eighty-seven-year-old leading lady had already been up for a couple of hours and then been driven out from Leeds before passing through the hands of wardrobe and make-up. On top of that the writer had handed her only five short words with which to paint the depth of the scene. Two Readys, two Spongos and a So.

And she had done it as only Thora could have done it, with the possible exception of my mother herself.

Now she was sitting on a cane chair in a light and airy conservatory. St Joseph's Residential Home was probably even older than Thora and yet it was playing the part of Springbank to perfection. You can't beat experience.

Alan Bell was due to shoot the scene in which my mother is about to be shown over the home by Noreen Kershaw, who is playing the part of Margaret.

In any biographical story of this nature there are bound to be scenes which bring back painful memories. Most of them would be pretty obvious to the viewer, but some are less obvious than others and this was one of them.

Not only was I about to 'put my mother away in a home', an action which left me running on empty for the next twelve months, but I was also acutely aware of how nervous she was. How she wanted to make a good impression.

By that time she could hardly string two sensible words together. When she was with the family, with Sally or Nick or Aileen or me, she could relax and laugh at herself, poke fun at herself, and then we could all settle down to the tedious task of trying to work out what the hell she was on about.

But here she was, setting out on yet another journey into the unknown and she wanted to prove herself. To show that she had dignity and was a woman of substance.

She had been quiet in the car and I knew she was

working on some sort of opening statement, some casual remark that would convince Margaret that they would indeed be lucky to have my mother as a resident in their home. She muttered away under her breath and put on her gracious face, which we always referred to as her Queen Mother look. So I left her to it.

We had sat in the hall for a few minutes, as Pete and Thora were doing now, waiting for Margaret to come and show us around. Every now and then we caught each other's eye and smiled nervously. She didn't want to talk. She was saving herself for the big moment.

Then Margaret appeared, ignoring me as she should. She went straight to my mother and sank down on her knees before her, taking both of her hands in hers.

'Mrs Longden. I've been looking forward to meeting you.'

My mother took a deep breath and then went for it, smiling her tight little Queen Mother's smile. Here it was, make or break.

'Yes, well it will have.'

She was so proud of herself. I could feel the relief flooding through her whole body. She'd done it. A whole sentence and she was sure it made sense. They wouldn't think she was some sort of idiot now. Not after that.

Alan Bell shouted action and Pete and Thora began to play out the scene. Noreen entered down a long hall, quickened her pace, and kneeled in front of Thora.

'Mrs Longden. I've been looking forward to meeting you.'

I began to wish I had spoken to Thora beforehand, to explain the state of my mother's mind at the time.

Thora smiled a sweet little smile, rather like that of the Queen Mother, and then, as if she were knighting

Noreen for services rendered, she took her voice slightly up-market towards posh.

'Yes, well it will have.'

I went out to the car for a cigarette and a think. I had some tissues on the back seat.

That was scene ninety-nine and from there we went straight into scene one hundred and four. They both took place in the conservatory and it would be easier to film them back to back rather than shift out the great mass of equipment and then lug it all back in again.

I was getting used to this business of shooting out of sequence. It made sense, of course, but I had often wondered how the actors coped. For instance, in a single morning Thora might have to take my mother's character on past the stroke to a point where she is beaten down and living in a confusing world that doesn't understand her any more, and then straight afterwards play her as an energetic and eccentric old lady who has a wonderful way with words. They were to film the stroke itself the following Wednesday afternoon.

It was a strange world that I had entered. That afternoon we would shoot the scene where Margaret takes my mother to show her Mrs Wibberley's room, so that she can see what can be done with a little imagination.

My mother falls in love with the room and Margaret and Pete become worried.

'Of course, this is Mrs Wibberley's room.'

But my mother doesn't understand and they almost have to drag her out. She wants that one. They take her across the landing to show her the room they have in mind for her. It's more like a hospital ward, bare and without frills and my mother wants nothing to do with it.

'Na. Crap. Ward – is a ward.'

Then Margaret calms her down and begins to paint a picture with her hands, showing her how it will look when it's furnished with all my mother's own belongings and gradually she draws her into the game.

The next scene is a dissolve. Time has passed and we see her in the room, nicely decorated, with her own bits and pieces all around her. The photographs are there on the sideboard along with so many of the other personal things we remember from her old house.

When it came to shooting the scenes Alan Bell filmed them in reverse order, simply because it would take the designers the best part of a day to furnish the room, but only twenty minutes for them to shift all the stuff out again.

That way, while the crew were busy filming in the conservatory, they could spend the whole morning arranging the props and then whip them all out again in the time it took Thora to change her costume. There would be little or no waiting around, and time was of the essence.

Perhaps somebody should have explained all this to the kitten. He must have spent hours in bed last night studying the script and now they were telling him that he was going to have to jump off the bed and walk out through the open door before he had even had a chance to come into the room.

It's a lot to ask of a kitten who hasn't done this sort of thing before and he panicked. First of all he jumped down off the counterpane and hid under the bed, and it took a whole posse of highly paid technicians to persuade him to come out.

They began by appealing to his better nature and then, when they discovered he didn't have one, they went under the bed after him, offering him handsome bribes, such as the corner of a ham sandwich, the top off a mayonnaise bottle and a kick up the backside. One of the crew told me that he'd had much the same experience while working with Dustin Hoffman.

Eventually the kitten got bored and wandered out. His handler grabbed him, sat him down and explained the situation in detail, and for the next five takes he jumped off the bed right on cue and just out of range of the camera.

Finally Thora managed to steer him in the right direction. He trotted down the length of the bed and hopped on to a coffee table. This wasn't in the script but we were prepared to let him wing it as long as he stayed in shot.

Then he disappeared under the bed once more and someone suggested that it might be kinder to have him put to sleep. Fortunately the camera was still running as his head emerged from under the counterpane. He paused momentarily, the frill of the bedspread framing his face so that he looked uncannily like the religious leader of some small Arab state. Then he was off across the carpet and out of the door.

It's not often you come across a kitten who has graduated from the method school of acting and this one had certainly been worth waiting for. By the time the furniture had been cleared and we were ready to shoot the scene before the one we had just shot, the kitten had worked out his motivation and had another surprise up his sleeve.

All he had to do was to appear in the open doorway, showing no sign whatsoever of the fact that his handler had just given him an almighty shove up the backside, and then march into the room.

This took a bit of doing and for the first few takes he

stopped in his tracks and turned round and glared at her.

'*Who the hell's the actor here, you or me?*'

Alan Bell left the two of them to sort it out. He has an acid tongue when it comes to working with human beings but when it comes to working with kittens he's a pussy cat.

'Action.'

This time the kitten came mincing round the door frame, more John Inman than John Wayne. He took two strides into the room, sat down, stuck his right back leg high in the air and began to lick his bottom outrageously.

'Cut.'

I think with a following wind and a bit of luck he might make it. There's a lot of talent there. With the right management and the right parts, who knows?

Let's just hope that Rolf Harris is watching when the film comes out.

We should have known. There is an old saying, never work with children or animals, but as far as I am aware no one has ever issued a warning about working with pottery.

In an earlier scene Penny Downie had been called upon to examine a china figurine. It was one of my mother's treasured possessions and the script asked for Thora to stroke it fondly, her fingers tracing the buttons on the shepherd boy's jacket, before handing it over to Penny.

Penny doesn't know that the head is loose, my mother having stuck it back on with the help of a matchstick and a great blob of Bostik.

As Penny lifts the figure up close to her eyes the head falls off and lands on the carpet.

MOTHER: It does that.
DERIC: They all do that.

It seemed an easy enough scene to shoot. With actors of Thora and Penny's calibre, a quick rehearsal and one take. That should do it.

But nobody had thought to rehearse the shepherd boy. We had to have a close-up of his head as it fell to the floor, bounced about a bit, and then lay still on the patterned carpet.

It took ages. For the first few attempts the head went straight under the sideboard and then the crew began to experiment with variations of back spin and side spin.

'Stick your fingers in his eyeballs and give him a flip.'

With practice they got closer and closer, but every time, as the head landed on the carpet, it would give one final death twitch and roll out of shot.

'Oh, sod it.'

You try it. Grab a camera, put your eye to the view-finder, and then drop a shepherd boy's head on the carpet. Now try to keep track of it as it lands. See what I mean?

It seemed to take for ever. Eventually the head was hurled to the floor in disgust and it must have realized it had pushed them too far. This time it did a nosedive, got its right ear caught in the tufted pile and lay where it had landed, absolutely knackered.

'Cut.'

Today we had to do it all over again, an echo of the previous shot. As my mother had her final stroke she would sweep the shepherd boy from the table and the ornament's symbolic fall would save Thora the trouble of taking a swallow dive herself. She's way past doing that sort of thing and it was a very small rug.

However, this time the figurine had to fall intact, come apart on impact, and then both the head and the body had to finish up close enough to each other so that the two of them would stay in the frame.

I left the crew to it and went for a cup of tea. I was getting wiser by the minute. I knew that after the first few abortive attempts a collective mutter would run round the room.

'Who wrote this bloody stuff?'

No point in telling them that it looked easy enough on paper. Much better to keep out of the way for a while.

It was a long, long while. I popped back every now and then and peeped round the door. They were getting nearer. At least the head was staying in the same room as the body. Best go and have another cup of tea, they'd get the hang of it eventually.

They were still at it when I left. I had rung Aileen and arranged to take her out for a meal. By the time I got home it would be too late to start cooking and over the past few weeks we'd had enough takeaway pizzas to last us a lifetime.

I was going to say goodbye to everyone, but as I walked up the corridor towards the set I heard Dave, the camera operator, shouting 'Sod it!' and I changed my mind. It's not that I'm a coward, I just don't like any unpleasantness.

Aileen was all dressed up and waiting for me to check her make-up.

'Well?'

We decided to calm down the bronzer a little, from an extremely healthy-looking Pocahontas to a more acceptable Gwyneth Paltrow.

'That's better.'

'Sure?'

'You look lovely.'

And she did. Black suits her flame-coloured hair wonderfully and once she had swapped the navy blue tights for a pair that matched her outfit she looked like a million dollars.

'Thanks.'

'My pleasure.'

We had a meal at the Birkby Lodge Hotel and I can highly recommend it. Not only because the business has been lovingly fashioned out of a wonderful old hall, with fantastic food and friendly service, but also because Gary, one of the owners, is an accomplished underwater hockey player.

I know. That's what I thought when he first told me. I asked him if he'd ever tried underwater table tennis or maybe deep sea ballooning, but apparently underwater hockey is for real.

They call it Octopush and it's played all over the world. They use a specially weighted puck and wear face masks, extra large fins and snorkels. Gary's so keen he goes training three nights a week, in Dewsbury, Miles Platting and Batley.

'The goal is ten foot wide and we have two refs.'

Perhaps everybody knows about it except me. Aileen said she thought she had heard of it before, but then she is the woman who once took part in a blind archery contest at county level and was disqualified for planting all of her six arrows in her opponent's target, so what does she know?

She also thought that it was the year of the buffalo in the Chinese calendar. I was sure it was the year of the rat and Gary suggested it might just be the year of the snake.

I can't for the life of me remember why it was important at the time or how it had come up in the first place, but it had and it was and on the way home Aileen was trying to work it out backwards. She counted out the years on her fingers.

'Rabbit, Gerbil, Hamster.'

Or something like that. Then I had a brilliant idea. We had just passed a Chinese takeaway, so I turned the car round and went in to consult the experts.

A pretty young Chinese girl was on duty. She looked about fifteen so she was probably twice that and married with three kids.

'Excuse me. Sorry to bother you, but I'm trying to settle an argument. Could you tell me what year it is in the Chinese calendar?'

It was late and she smiled a tired smile that told me she had already dealt with more than enough plonkers for one night.

'You wan menu?'

'No, I just wondered if you could tell me what year it is.'

'Wha year?'

'Yes.'

The inscrutable smile became a little less scrutable.

'Wan moment plis.'

And with that she disappeared through a curtain of plastic strips and within seconds it sounded as though World War Three had just broken out in the kitchen. Voices were raised to fever pitch and at one point a man's face poked out between the plastic ribbons for a good long look at me. Then there came an unnerving silence, eventually broken by the girl's delicate steps as she hurried to put me out of my misery.

'Sorry keep you.'

'That's all right.'

'Cook says year is 1999.'

'Thank you very much.'

I thanked her again before I left. She said it was no problem and took the weight off her feet by leaning against the counter, waiting for the next prat to come prancing in through the door. To those in the trade it's all part and parcel of that troublesome hour between midnight and one in the morning.

Aileen asked me how I had got on.

'Apparently it's 1999.'

She was still laughing by the time we got home. Maybe it's the year of the hyena.

Chapter Fifteen

Tigger was on guard by the laundry basket. She sits there for hours, waiting for the washing to begin. Then she insists on sniffing each and every garment before it is hurled deep into the bowels of the washing machine. It's a sort of feline quality control and she's very good at it.

She doesn't sniff them on the way out as she has become allergic to Sainsbury's meadow-fresh fabric conditioner. It makes her eyes water and she says she can't taste her tuna for days afterwards.

While Aileen held out a lace-trimmed pillow case for her to sample I took Kealen and Claire to the upstairs kitchen to show them the ropes. They had offered to look after the house for us while we were away for the weekend and I knew it would be in safe hands.

They would also be cat-sitting and here one or two doubts were poised at the back of my mind. So I tried to make everything crystal clear.

'Thermal and William like the tuna in water, but Tigger prefers the smaller tins in brine. They're the tins on the second shelf and she has smaller portions than the other two – if you give her too much she won't touch it. They all have their own likes and dislikes, and so I've marked the tins of cat food with an indelible pencil: with a "TH" for Thermal and a single "T" for Tigger. William's are marked with a "W".'

Kealen turned this information over in her mind.

'Let me see now. Thermal is the white one, isn't he?'

I wondered for a moment if I should mark each of the cats with an indelible pencil, but decided it would be going a little too far.

'The coley steaks go in the microwave for three minutes and then I let them stand for a while. The cats prefer them hot, but not too hot. So I blow on them and then I . . .'

At this point I glanced at Kealen and her eyes were telling me that once I was out of the way these blessed cats would eat whatever they were damn well given and be grateful for it.

To be on the safe side I had written out a long list of instructions, but there were one or two other things that I needed to point out, for instance that Thermal liked to sleep in my office and that I always left him a midnight snack on my desk, just to the right of the letter rack. Also that I changed their water daily – using the filter tap in the kitchen, not the ordinary tap.

The more I told them the dafter I felt, but I just couldn't stop myself. I mentioned in passing that Tigger slept on the fax machine in Aileen's office and asked them not to draw the curtains, otherwise she wouldn't be able to see the cars going past in the night, and that William liked to sleep in the kitchen, with his chin hanging over the edge of his feeding bowl, to save time in the morning.

I had filled two sheets of A4 paper with instructions and, as Kealen skimmed through them I watched her eyebrows going up and down like a pair of Venetian blinds.

'How long are you going for?'

'Just the weekend.'

She passed the sheets over to Claire. Claire has a way with words – she clubs people to death with them.

'What about their ballet lessons?'

We had only been driving for a couple of miles when Aileen pushed back her seat and settled down for a nap.

'Sorry about this.'

'That's all right.'

She can't cope with the bends as we drive through Flockton and on towards the M1. Because she can't see where we are going they tend to make her feel dizzy and sick.

'I'll just have five minutes.'

That means I've lost her for the next ninety miles. Once she has dropped off she could snooze her way through a multiple pile-up, but somehow she always manages to wake up just two miles short of the Leicester Forest East service station.

'What about a cup of coffee?'

No matter how hard I try I have never been able to smuggle her past that point and it's becoming an obsession with me. Once, for one glorious moment, I thought I had cracked it. I played one of the relaxation tapes she'd brought back with her from an aromatherapy session, all pan-pipes and water music, trickling streams and babbling brooks. Another half mile and I would have done it. But just before we reached Leicester Forest East she shot up and snapped back the seat.

'I need to go to the toilet.'

*   *   *

But today I was in with a chance. We were going to Stratford-upon-Avon which meant turning off the M1 and on to the M42, several miles short of Leicester Forest East. Let's see if she could sort that one out.

Did I tell you that Nick and Lisa now own a restaurant cruiser which they have moored on the Avon at Stratford? Well, I should have done. It's called *The Countess of Evesham* and it's rather like the Orient Express with water wings, all brass fittings and deep rich wood.

They have had it for almost three years now and they cruise up the river and back for three hours, lunchtime and evenings, serving up great food and wonderful scenery.

They've survived a complete lack of experience and several great dollops of really bad luck, not least the disastrous floods of Easter '97 when Nick spent twenty-four hours up to his waist in water, hanging on to his business for grim life.

Now they have it down to a fine art and I couldn't be more thrilled for them. I always wanted a son with a restaurant. What could be better than to be the father of mine host, sitting at a table in a quiet corner, being plied with fresh food and fine wines?

Aileen and I were there the week they opened and on the way down I told her that I would insist on paying my way. 'They can't afford to give free meals away, not at this stage.'

But knowing how generous my son is, I knew I was in for a stiff battle.

As we boarded I took him to one side.

'Look, Nick. I insist on paying.'

He escorted us both to our table.

'You bloody well will,' he told me. 'We can't be doing with any freeloaders, not at this stage.'

*   *   *

Aileen slept like a baby all the way there. Her nostrils quivered slightly as we whipped past a Little Chef on the A46, but it obviously didn't have the pulling power of the Leicester Forest East service station and so, after a bit of a sniff and a brief nostril-to-nostril consultation the two of them decided it wasn't worth waking her up. She slept on while they kept a lookout for something a little more enticing.

Just outside Stratford we passed a hitchhiker sitting on the grass verge. He had propped himself up against a tree and had a rough cardboard sign leaning against his knees.

KID.

He didn't look much of a kid to me and it was a mile or so further on before it dawned on me that he must have been trying to get a lift to Kidderminster. I wouldn't have picked him up anyway. You can't nowadays, can you? The men might mug you and the women might claim to have been raped, although there's a better than even chance that it could be the other way around.

And to think of the chances I've taken in the past. A young man who I thought was ill – he certainly wasn't drunk – who I now realize was out of his mind on drugs. A teenage girl who wobbled along on stiletto heels that were high enough to have given her vertigo and who asked if she could sit in the back, where she promptly whipped off her mini-dress and pulled on a pair of jeans and a T-shirt that she had tucked away in a plastic bag.

'Me mam thinks I've been out with our Glenys.'

It's a shame. I've learned a lot from hitchhikers over the years, not least that if you lend them any money you never get it back. But I think even I would have made an exception for a girl I read about recently. She was standing on the hard shoulder of the A1, holding up a large well-printed sign.

I HAVE CHOCOLATE.

You couldn't say no, could you?

The boat was filling up nicely by the time we arrived and Aileen woke as fresh as a daisy.

'Did I snore?'

'No.'

'Good.'

She's never got over waking up from a deep sleep at a set of traffic lights in Droylsden one Sunday morning. A cyclist was leaning on the car door, staring in at her through the passenger window. I tapped her on the knee.

'What?'

'You had your mouth wide open and there's a kid looking in at you.'

Ever since then she's managed to organize her subconscious so that she sleeps with her mouth fashioned into a tight little rosebud. It looks ever so cute and I'm glad I didn't tell her that the kid had probably never even noticed.

She also had the top three buttons of her shirt undone and the view was truly stupendous. It had kept me going for the past fifty miles, but it was almost the end of the kid on the bike.

When we set off he wasn't concentrating and we took him with us. He was trapped between my car and the car on the inside lane, and as we both slowed down to let him out, he shot forward and was almost emasculated by a couple of wing mirrors. He didn't seem too upset about it at the time. I know it's a price I would willingly have paid myself.

*   *   *

The boat was full and the passengers seemed very happy and relaxed as we set off out of the marina. Everyone except me, that is. I was due to talk to the assembled company for forty minutes on the return trip and already I was beginning to panic.

An Evening with Deric Longden. That's what it said on the menu. Nick hadn't had the space to print the full title of the event.

An evening with Deric Longden, together with a full supporting cast of a thousand mallards, hundreds of swans and various other waterfowl, all of whom will be performing cute little tricks right outside your window as he talks.

That's not to mention the locks. I knew I was going to have difficulty in holding the guests' attention and I had anticipated the problems that might be presented by the ever-changing scenery, but hadn't thought for a moment about the locks.

I never have to worry about passing through locks when I am about to perform in some distant outpost of the Hilton Hotel chain. As long as the microphone is working properly and the audience are pointing in roughly the right direction, I can usually hold their attention, whatever else the gods might throw at me. But locks?

I had my first taste of what was in store for me in the canal lock, and that was before we had even hit the river. The huge gates were opened wide and in we sailed. There were only a few inches to spare on either side of the boat and half a dozen swans, who had decided to come along for the ride, wisely stayed up near the pointy bit at the front where they would have a little more room.

The water rushed out of the lock and the boat

descended, or rather the walls seemed to grow to a great height all around us. The diners sat at their tables, staring out of the windows and sipping their first drink of the evening. Then a woman up near the pointy bit became rather agitated.

'The swans, they're going to be killed!'

Of course they were in no danger whatsoever. They knew what they were doing. They would just get swished about a bit as the swell of the water carried them this way and that.

'Let's have a spot of fun with 'em.'

'Go on then. You first.'

One of the smaller swans made a dash for it, the length of the boat, from pointy bit to blunt bit, flapping his wings in sheer terror.

'Please help me. I am but a poor swan about to be crushed to death.'

The others joined in the flurry of wing flapping, hardly daring to look.

'Help him. He can't swim.'

The swan put on an even better performance on his way back towards his mates, this time incorporating his famous broken-wing impression that always goes down so well with the tourists.

Then, once they had wound us up, they turned their elegant backs on us in disgust, bobbing up and down majestically until the gates were opened wide enough to let them out on to the river.

My heart fell and my confidence came out in sympathy. How the hell do you compete with that? Aileen, of course, hadn't seen any of this.

'Let's go up front for a smoke.'

I joined her and did my best to paint a picture of the Avon for her as we cruised past the Royal Shakespeare Theatre and Holy Trinity Church.

*   *   *

How Mark manages to produce such wonderful food from his tiny galley I shall never know. He's an excellent chef and a qualified skipper and you don't get many of those to the pound. He's also a brave man. He had duck on the menu, so Nick was the skipper today, up on top, taking us safely through the locks and keeping a weather eye open for protest groups of marauding mallards.

After the starter and main course we moored up at Lullington for a while, so that we could stretch our legs while Nick turned the boat around.

Lisa introduced me to Scruffy, the local duck. The name is appropriate – she's a bag lady of a duck whose feathers don't try hard enough. They each have a mind of their own and seem to be in a state of continual dispute with one another.

Scruffy shuns the bright lights of Stratford, preferring the quiet of the countryside. But she likes a bit of company every now and then and as soon as the boat docked she jumped on board and settled herself above the hatch, quacking a raucous welcome to each and every diner as they made their way off the boat.

She went missing last year and then, much to Lisa's relief, just as they thought they would never see her again, she reappeared with a line of five little ducklings, one of whom Nick bravely saved from the attentions of an angry swan.

Scruffy has been eternally grateful ever since and she loves him dearly, which is at least something, since the swan also remembers him and lays siege to his private parts whenever she sets eyes on him.

The light began to fade as we set out on the return journey and my spirits started to rise. Maybe I would get away with it after all. Then the floodlights came on and lit the river banks with magic. Performing mallards waited until they were highlighted in a convenient cross-beam before sticking their heads in the water and their bums high in the air.

I got away with it, just. Mainly because the *Countess of Evesham* was full of decent people that night, who tried hard to pretend that there wasn't a swan peering in at them through the table window, that we weren't rising spectacularly in yet another lock and that there was nothing funny at all about that mallard who was mooning at us. He was just being rude and we shouldn't encourage him.

So I kept it short and then afterwards they were all able to relax. As we returned to the basin, with Holy Trinity Church gloriously floodlit behind us, the birds were beginning to settle down for the night.

The ducks were plastered all along the river bank, miles of them lined up like shuttlecocks, six inches apart, and the latecomers were belting up and down the river looking for a space.

'*I was there last night.*'

'*Bugger off.*'

The swans had their own special island, dozens of them reclining graciously under the delicate umbrella of a weeping willow.

It was all so beautiful and I began to relax as well. I had got through the talk without being lynched and signed an awful lot of books afterwards. Liz, the head waitress, brought me a large whisky and suddenly I felt very hungry. I could really have enjoyed my dinner now.

We sat up talking most of the night and the next morning I woke with a thumping great headache and a small white cat fast asleep on my chest.

'Come on, Bart, give us a break.'

She's a strange cat. Nick found her wandering alone in Dubai and brought her home with him when he came back from the Emirates. He named her after Bart Simpson and then found out later that she was a girl. Her hobby is sitting on your chest and staring blankly straight in your face. It's quite unnerving, she never blinks. I picked her up and plonked her on the bedside rug.

'Stay there. I'm going for a shower.'

It's not possible for her to sit on your chest while you are having a shower so she just sits on the bath mat and stares, but not necessarily straight in your face.

'Stop staring, Bart. It's rude.'

If Dougal from *The Magic Roundabout* had been a cat, then Bart could have played him to perfection. She's a mobile mop of white silky fur with no discernible legs and no undercarriage, just two enormous black eyes that seem to see straight through you.

'I shan't tell you again.'

The bathroom door swung open and Lisa marched in.

'Is Bart bothering you?'

'She just keeps staring at me.'

Lisa bent and scooped up the cat from the bath mat.

'How many times have I told you? It's rude to stare.'

My beautiful daughter-in-law then draped herself all along the side of the bath.

'What do you fancy for breakfast?'

'A slice of toast will do.'

'We've got bacon and eggs.'

'No, it's all right. Just toast and coffee. Be fine.'

I soaped a bit here and I soaped a bit there and listened intently as Lisa told me how Bart had this very bad habit of wandering into the bathroom and embarrassing their friends. She tapped the cat on the nose.

'And it's very naughty.'

She stood up and made for the door, then turned with the cat staring back at me from over her shoulder.

'Right then, just toast and coffee?'

'That'll be lovely.'

'Come on then, Bart. Let's get cracking. And for goodness' sake, stop staring.'

She tapped the cat on the nose once more as they went out.

'I don't know where you get it from.'

I think I do.

Chapter Sixteen

We were home by lunchtime and the cats were strung out in a line on the garden wall waiting for us. I told Aileen and she went over to say hello.

But they jumped down and marched up the drive ahead of us, ignoring us completely, dodging under our vain attempts at back-scratching and meeting our fond greetings with a stony glare.

Once inside Thermal went straight into the lounge and jumped on Kealen's knee, purring like an outboard motor, while Tigger gave a great big stretch and then curled herself up around Claire's feet. William marched stiffly into the kitchen and lay down on the floor with his chin resting miserably on the lip of his empty dish.

It's always the same if we leave them for more than a few hours.

'Stuff you, then.'

But Aileen isn't one for confrontations and she dug deep into her handbag. We had saved them a sausage each from the Little Chef on the way home and as William was the nearest he got first choice.

After a few moments the other two drifted in from the lounge, like Bisto kids sniffing the air, and then they began purring and rubbing round our legs. We stuck it out for as long as we could, but eventually our resistance crumbled. Still, it's nice to be wanted for yourself, isn't it?

I left Aileen to unpack and nipped over to Roundhay Park in Leeds. Earlier in the film schedule we had shot a scene in Greenhead Park, almost opposite my study window. Thora and Pete were seated on a bench and Thora was telling him that she wouldn't sell up her house and come to live with him.

MOTHER: I don't think so, love.
DERIC: Why not?
MOTHER: Oh, I could write you a list as long as your arm. I've done it, you know, four sisters – one after another. I finished up hating our Jessie.

The scene took a long time to set up and the light wasn't all that promising and so while they were hanging about I went off to help find a suitable site for the last shot of the day.

Rather than spend time going all the way over to Chesterfield, the props department had decided to bring Chesterfield over to Huddersfield and they had a huge sign in the back of the van.

Welcome to Chesterfield. A fine market town.

All we needed now was a straight stretch of road with a soft grass verge in which to plant the sign and within minutes we could shift Chesterfield forty-five miles up the M1 to Yorkshire.

It took longer than I thought it might, but eventually we found a spot that would fill the bill, on the Brighouse road into Huddersfield.

And it worked very well indeed. After the scene on

the park bench was all done and dusted, Pete would come up here, drive down the road, see the sign, glance at his watch and look worried.

Unfortunately between the planting of the sign and the shooting of the scene a lot of other drivers would see the sign, glance at their watches and look worried.

They had just left Brighouse on their way to Huddersfield and now here they were, on the outskirts of Chesterfield. Maps would be pulled out of glove compartments and brows furrowed.

By the time I had got back to Greenhead Park the scene on the bench was already in the can and Aileen was none too happy. She had worked as my script associate all the way through the writing of the play and knew exactly what I had in mind for every line of every scene.

'Alan asked Thora to break down and cry at the end of the bread and butter line.'

And that wasn't what I had in mind at all. The scene finishes with my mother springing a surprise on me.

MOTHER: No. I've made up my mind. I've found a place. One of them residential homes. You've got your own room and they look after you very well. And you can have as much bread and butter as you want.

They get up to leave.

DERIC: But there's no need . . .

MOTHER (*interrupting*): I can't remember what it was called offhand.

Deric goes back to the bench for her handbag.

DERIC: We're noted for our bread and butter, you know. They come from miles around.

Cut to interior of church hall.

On the surface the whole point of this scene, in fact of the whole play, is that each of them wants what is best for the other. The subtext, however, is a different matter altogether.

Deric has already spent fifteen years nursing his first wife until her death two years ago and now, just as he has begun to forge a whole new life for himself, it looks as though he is going to be saddled all over again, this time with the burden of caring for his mother at first hand.

Because he loves her dearly he is prepared to take her in and look after her and he continues to make this quite clear. But in his heart of hearts he hopes that she will insist on going into a residential home. It would take the pressure off him. After all he couldn't blame himself, could he? He had done his level best to persuade her. And it was what she wanted – wasn't it?

At the same time his mother knows full well that she can't live on her own for much longer, but she dreads the idea of giving up her independence and retiring into a communal home. Yet she is determined not to be a burden on her son and turns down his offer again and again. However, if he continues to push her for much longer – who knows?

It's a drama that is forever being played out in family after family, right across the land.

'You've got your own room and they look after you very well. And you can have as much bread and butter as you want.'

That last sentence, however daft it sounds, was meant to show how difficult it was for her to come up with anything really positive about the prospect of living in a home, and Deric realizes this. She was being brave in spite of everything and if she had broken down and cried at that moment, then the game would have been

215

up and there is no way that he could have ever let it happen.

I know, because I was there.

But Alan Bell thought differently and he was very excited about the way Thora had responded to his direction.

'There won't be a dry eye in the house.'

'But I don't want them crying at that point.'

'Just wait until you see it.'

'It's going to make Deric look an absolute bastard.'

I had become quite used to referring to myself in the third person. I switched easily between Deric, Pete and Him.

'You'll love it when you see it.'

But I didn't. It was too much, too early, and fortunately the producers agreed with me and insisted that we do it all over again.

These things happen. Right at the end of the film Thora is in hospital, unable to communicate in any recognizable way, and Pete is sitting on the edge of her bed. Two young nurses, wonderfully played by Jennifer Luckcraft and Katisha Kenyon, are examining a photograph of my mother taken in Blackpool when she was a young woman. I had brought it in so that they could see that she was a real person with an interesting past and not just a bag of bones in a hospital bed.

NURSE 1: Who's this? Is it her daughter?

DERIC: No. It's my mother. When she was young.

NURSE 1: Really? I love that coat. They're in again, aren't they? I was looking at one just like it in Next not long ago. Couldn't afford it though.

Nurse No. 2 enters and glances over her colleague's shoulder.

NURSE 1: Mrs Longden. When she was young.

NURSE 2: Where was this taken?

DERIC: Blackp—

NURSE 1 (*interrupting*): It's Paris. There's that tower, look.

DERIC: She travelled a lot.

Mother has no idea what is going on. Nurse 2 sits on the edge of mother's bed and shows her the photograph.

DERIC: Modelling, you know.

Mother recognizes herself and is pleased. But she has no idea what is being said.

MOTHER: Dobbie.

NURSE 2: And you were a model in Paris?

MOTHER: Oh merrily.

NURSE 2: Wow. And did you mix with all them famous painters?

MOTHER (*nods seriously*): They came at it.

NURSE 2: Wow.

NURSE 1 (*taking the photo*): I love that coat.

She lays the photograph wistfully on the bed.

NURSE 1: Course it's how you wear 'em, isn't it?

As the two nurses talk, the camera closes in on the photograph.

Cut to interior of mother's new house.

The next scene takes us back, through the photograph, to the beginning of the play, to where Pete is sorting through my mother's meagre possessions. He takes out her purse, glances inside, and then produces a few coins.

'Didn't pay much, did it? Modelling.'

I had been very proud of this smooth transition from past to present, but Alan added a personal touch of genius to the scene. As the photograph was laid on the bed he closed in on Thora's hand and we watched it slowly move across the counterpane until it gently covered her son's.

In that one wonderful moment he had shown that although she had no idea of what was going on, she knew that something had changed and whatever it was, it was working in her favour.

It was absolutely right and it was Alan's doing, not mine. There wasn't a dry eye in the cutting room as we ran the scene over and over again.

We reshot the bench scene in Roundhay Park in Leeds to save time. The crew were filming nearby and given a handy tree, a stretch of grass and a wooden bench, one park can be made to look very much like another. This time Thora simply gave Pete a wistful smile at the end, a brave little smile that said everything that had to be said. No lace handkerchief and no tears.

To this day Alan and Thora still think they had the scene right first time. Pete didn't and I didn't and more importantly the producers didn't. You win some, you lose some, but I'm glad we won that one.

On the way home I had some shopping to do. Man the hunter, stalking the aisles of an out-of-town Tesco in search of fresh food.

They had grapefruit on offer, buy two and get one free. I bought twelve of them and completely filled my basket, so I swopped it for a trolley the size of an articulated lorry and the two of us ploughed our way across the store.

I added a huge bag of over-ripe pears for juicing with the grapefruit and congratulated myself on the fact that with my trolley already half full we now had enough fruit juice to see us through the next six days.

Cat litter was also on offer. It came in a thumping great gro-bag of a thing that was full of wood chippings and would take two men to lift it, always assuming, of course, that I was one of the two men.

'Let me give you a hand.'

He must have been eighty. It would now take three men to lift it, always assuming that he and I were two of the three men.

'No, it's all right, really. I can manage.'

'You take that end.'

I took that end and he took the other, but it was jammed against the shelf above and we had to shuffle a load of stuff sideways and then out into the aisle before we could even make a start.

We pushed the bag over on to its side, and then with knees and stomachs and thighs and at least one rather delicate crotch, we pulled it outwards and lifted it skywards and then dumped it in the trolley.

It landed on the grapefruit and pears with an ominous squelch and it occurred to me that I might have achieved a personal best. I was already juicing the fruit before I had even left the store. Then a trickle of wood chippings filtered out of a torn corner of the bag to add a distinctive, sort of crunchy quality to the sticky mixture. Mmm, yummy.

I couldn't think what had possessed me to buy such a monster, but never mind. It would see me out. I could top up the cats' litter trays for many years to come and never have to leave the house. And if there were any left over I could always insulate the loft.

The old man was leaning against the shelf, breathing

heavily, but quietly content with the past few minutes of his life.

'Bet you can't guess how old I am?'

Oh I hate it when they say that. If you get it spot on they are sorely disappointed and if you go over the top they are downright offended.

'I'm afraid I'm not very good at that sort of thing.'

'Go on. See if you can guess?'

So while I was down on my knees, clearing the aisle and restacking the shelf, I had a guess, and then took away the number I first thought of.

'Sixty-seven.'

He beamed. He had glanced in the mirror before coming out that morning and could well understand my making such a mistake. He pushed himself away from the support of the shelf and stood there straight-backed, rocking gently on his own two feet.

'I'm eighty-six. And I've never had a terminal illness in my life.'

We met up again a few aisles further on. Man the hunter had now added a twelve-pack of Andrex toilet rolls to his trolley and was in danger of becoming seriously overloaded. If I had been out on the road the police would have asked me to pull over.

I hauled the trolley over towards the more exotic sauces and concentrates. Whenever I run out of ideas I select a jar at random and then read the recipe suggestion on the label. This time it was Patak's Original Balti Curry Paste and I was making a note that I now needed plain yoghurt, tomatoes and eight ounces of chicken, when I heard the old man grumbling down by the pasta sauce.

'Foreign muck.'

I edged my way towards him.

'What are you after?'

'HP sauce.'

It was up at the far end of the aisle. I had passed it as I turned sharp left at kitchen rolls and had noticed that they were clean out of the fruity variety. HP sauce, that is – not kitchen rolls.

'Come with me.'

So far he had only the one item in his basket.

'Did you know that's balsamic vinegar you've got there?'

'It's all right, isn't it? They didn't have any Sarson's.'

'I'm sure they have. Let's have a look.'

We strode on through the retail jungle, man the hunter and his ancient sidekick.

'Bet you can't guess how old I am?'

'Eighty-six.'

The disappointment flooded his face.

'You told me back there.'

'Oh that were you, were it?'

I sorted him out with the sauce and the vinegar.

'Right. That's me done. I'll stop off for some fish and chips on my way home.'

I still had the jar of balti paste in my hand and I checked the recipe to see if I needed anything else.

'My brother used to mess about with all that sort of stuff. He were a devil for that pasta rubbish.'

A tremor of revulsion ran the length of his spine.

'Have you ever tried it raw? It's horrible.'

I had actually. I once bit into one of those multi-coloured shell-shaped things. It was horrible.

'He swore by it. Healthy living and video exercises every morning and he only lived to be seventy-nine. That Jane Fonda's got a lot to answer for.'

*   *   *

The traffic on the M62 was at a standstill and the boredom on the way home was only slightly relieved by random thoughts of a seventy-nine-year-old man doing exercises to a Jane Fonda video.

The car stopped in front of me was suffering badly, with steam pouring out from under the bonnet. A young woman in her mid-twenties jumped out of the driver's seat and tried to delay the inevitable by pouring a small bottle of Malvern water into the radiator.

It wasn't really up to the task. This wasn't part of the job specification. When the bottle left the factory it had been led to believe that it was destined for better things than this. Smart dinner parties with the chattering classes, perhaps, or working hand in hand with some thrusting young executive, forever on the move. Anything but this – and as she poured the water into the radiator it went all weak at the knees and turned into steam at the very thought.

While the young woman obviously wasn't born to be a motor mechanic she had certainly been born to wear jeans and as she bent and puzzled over the radiator a dozen pairs of eyes watched her closely as the traffic began to move.

I was the first to offer help, but by the time she had settled herself in the driving seat there were about nine of us milling around. Four of them set about man-handling the car from fast lane to hard shoulder, while the rest of us held back the traffic to make sure her path was clear.

I pulled over in front of her while she used my mobile phone to ring the RAC and then, having made sure she was going to be all right, I gave her a wave and eased myself back into the traffic.

We would have done it for anyone, of course, but a good bum doesn't half speed things up.

*   *   *

The balti chicken was a great success, even though I say so myself. I had spiced up the stir-fry with flesh from the grapefruit, and the rice was light and fluffy. The naan breads were just about perfect, despite the fact that they looked more like a couple of heavily muscled odour-eaters.

I wish I could say the same for the cat litter. I had hauled it in from the car and dragged it down the cellar steps, leaving a tell-tale trail of wood chips behind me.

After I had swept it up I emptied each of the three personalized litter trays from upstairs, together with the all-comers' communal skip in the cellar, then washed them out and dried them off, refilling the whole bunch of them with the sweet-smelling wood chips.

I showed Thermal my handiwork. He had a good sniff and then backed off.

'*What the hell is it?*'

'They're natural wood chips.'

'*What was wrong with the other stuff?*'

'I thought we'd try something new.'

'*We?*'

'Well, you – and the others.'

But they wouldn't go anywhere near it. William jumped in his tray, had a quick nibble and then jumped out again.

'*Tastes funny.*'

'You're not supposed to eat it.'

Tigger took one look and ran out of the room. I couldn't think what could be wrong with it and I was just about to ask Aileen for a second opinion when the doorbell rang.

It was Mrs Cartwright from down the road. She took up most of the doorway and, backlit by the outside light, her shadow painted the mosaic tiled floor a solid black until eventually it ran out of puff and gave up, over by the combined boot-scraper and umbrella stand.

'I'm fed up to the teeth with them,' she blustered. 'They're forever in my garden. They camp there all afternoon like a bunch of boy scouts.'

I promised to do what I could – though I didn't know what I could do. Confiscate Thermal's Swiss-army knife perhaps, or threaten to readjust Little Chap's toggle if ever he set foot on Mrs Cartwright's lawn again?

'I can't keep them on a lead, you know.'

'Well, if I catch them at it once more, I'll set the dog on them.'

She stormed off down the path. I managed to keep a straight face until I had closed the door tight behind her and shut myself in the kitchen.

Set the dog on them. Have you seen her dog? No, of course you haven't – that's a silly question. It's one of those miniature white poodles. He's had his middle shaved like a belly dancer, wears a couple of pairs of sculpted plus-fours and has a stringy little tail with a great big furry bobble on the end.

I know it's not the dog's fault and I know that, despite being made to look a right Charlie by their owners, some of these poodles are very tough little devils indeed. I suppose they have to be, looking like that – but not this one.

His name is Buffy and he's still suffering nightmares from having once barked at Tigger in what he supposed to be an aggressive fashion.

'*I beg your pardon. Are you addressing me by any chance?*'

'*Woof.*'

He never knew what hit him. One minute he was poncing down the path like a Vivienne Westwood

224

model and the next he was upside down in the catmint with a very sore nose and an ego to match.

It's the catmint of course that draws the cats over there, time after time. There are acres of the stuff, completely surrounding a huge sunken lawn that hosts a rustic bird table and an old stone birdbath and is at all times covered with the crumbs of at least four loaves of bread with the crusts cut off, for those older birds who have lost their teeth and are afraid of heights.

And it's the ideal spot for my four furry ornithologists to spend a sunny summer's afternoon. They lie on their backs, soaking up the sun and breathing in the catmint.

'Hey, man – this is the real stuff.'

Buffy glares fiercely from the other side of the French windows, his mouth opening and shutting silently as he yelps at them from behind the safety of the double glazing.

'Yeah. Roll me another joint. That dog over there's beginning to look damned attractive. Just love those cute little pyjamas.'

They rarely catch a bird. About once a year they come across an ancient sparrow, an old-age pensioner complete with Zimmer frame, who just happens to be studying a pamphlet on euthanasia at the time, but generally they are far too stoned on the catmint to give a damn about anything as active as hunting, shooting or fishing.

I wish I had trained them properly, but it's too late now. They are set in their ways, even when it comes to a change of cat litter.

I thought of Henry and wondered how Thermal might have turned out if I had been more forceful with him when he was a kitten.

'Who's Henry?'

'He's an actor. He has to sit still for ages and then

jump over a settee when his trainer gives him a signal. Then he has to jump off a sink.'

'*What's the money like?*'

'Pretty good.'

'*I could have done that.*'

'No, you couldn't. You would have run off and hidden in the scenery. Anyway – you're the wrong colour.'

'*That's racial discrimination, that is.*'

'Don't be ridiculous.'

'*I could have you for that.*'

But I don't think I need to worry. One word from me and the police will have him for being in possession of catmint with a street value of over twenty-three pence. They'd lock him up and throw away the key.

It's a tough business, show business. Even if you do sleep with the writer.

Chapter Seventeen

Next morning the birds burst into song at six o'clock on the dot. They don't know that we put the clocks forward a couple of months ago and by rights I should have been enjoying an extra hour's unbroken sleep.

The trouble is that now I wake up at five o'clock on the dot and simply lie there in bed, waiting for them to get ready for their early morning session, while they clean their teeth, wash their hair and shave their legs or whatever.

Mind you, I don't think this pair have started shaving anything yet. They are just a couple of kids. The long one and the short one have disappeared, flown off to the exotic east, Cleethorpes or Skegness or somewhere, to enjoy the sun and the sand and the donkey rides.

The newcomers are at that awkward stage, teenagers who think that pretending to be bored out of their skulls is somehow interesting.

'*Coo . . . ool.*'

That's about all I get out of them and one day soon I'm going to climb up there on the roof and give them a good kick up the bum.

No more imaginative mobile phone impressions and

no more selections from the best of light opera, just a monosyllabic rap that goes on and on until I feel like chewing the duvet.

'*Hey man – like wow.*'

I should have taken the short one under my wing when I had the chance and encouraged him to extend his repertoire. He could have had a crack at the fax machine and the whistling kettle. He might have made it on television.

'*When I return, Matthew, I shall be – a smoke alarm.*'

However there is one bright spark on the horizon or, to be more accurate, on the other side of the third tall chimney pot on the main roof, the one with the twisted cowl that's neither use nor ornament. I haven't seen him yet but I imagine he wears glasses. He's not one for joining in and he waits until the others have packed away their gear and moved on to their next gig.

He is still only in the rehearsal stage, you understand, but he's working very hard on a more than passable rendition of 'You can't touch me, I'm part of the union'. We'll have to wait and see if he has the staying power, and then of course he's going to need that all-important lucky break. But with a little more practice and a decent backing group he could turn out to be the best of the bunch.

On our way over to the studio Aileen and I stopped off at Wakefield to see Goldie Armitage. She's a much loved friend of ours, but nowadays it's not a trip that we take lightly.

She is in a nursing home, just as my mother was, and going through pretty much the same living hell that Thora would be painfully recreating in a church hall over in Leeds at this very moment.

It wasn't always this way. Goldie was once the life

228

and soul of any party, with a voice like a gravel pit and an endless fund of risqué stories that would curl the hair of the uninitiated.

She also had an indomitable spirit and a laugh that could strip wallpaper at fifty yards. Goldie was the sort of person who brought something extra into the lives of all who knew her. And then she had a series of strokes.

'I wonder how she'll be today?'

It was a question hardly worth the asking. Nowadays she can do nothing for herself, she has to be fed and dressed and bathed and her conversation has been whittled down until it is little more than a grunt. We rarely understand what she is trying to say to us and I'm sure she has no idea what the hell we are on about.

And so we all smile at one another until it hurts and we are all so bloody jolly until Goldie, who has more sense than the rest of us, cries at the awfulness of it and then we are all so solemn. We adjust her pillow and massage her shoulders and tell her stories about her old friends. She doesn't understand, but we tell her anyway.

Last year Aileen and I drove her to a writers' week at Swanwick, in Derbyshire. She had been going there for donkey's years and she would be among old friends who would remember her as the woman she was and not have to start from scratch.

And it all worked out very well. Carol, her carer, took the brunt of the load and we all pitched in, her wheel-chair burning up the corridors and leaving scorch marks on the grass.

She tired towards the end of the week, but still her face lit up at seeing so many faces from the past and with the intelligent use of her eyebrows, the odd grunt here and there and an extremely dirty laugh, she attempted a strangled conversation with all and sundry.

One morning we were sitting quietly at a table in the

Vinery, soaking up the sunshine and indulging in a death or glory battle with the writers Mary Wibberley and Jolante to see who would be first to complete the *Daily Telegraph* cryptic crossword.

This isn't fun, it's war, and it's been rumbling on for as long as I can remember. Once upon a time Goldie was one of the foot soldiers, but today she was merely an observer, her wheelchair pulled up close as she stared into the middle distance.

I have to read the clues out loud to Aileen and Mary does her best to irritate us.

'Oh, we got that one ages ago.'

Mary is very good at irritating people, she's been doing it for years, but she kept quiet as I read out the clue to thirteen across.

'. . . and it's six letters.'

Aileen worked at it in her head, Jolante scribbled something in the margin of the newspaper and I tried to look intelligent. And then from Goldie's wheelchair there came a deep robotic growl.

'En-ig-ma.'

I went as cold as ice. Mary took it in her stride.

'You were quick there, Goldie. Beat the lot of us.'

I shall never forget the look of joy on Goldie's face that morning. For one moment she had cut through the fog. She shuffled in her chair and bent over towards us, listening intently as I read out clue after clue. We held some of the answers back in the hope that she might double her score, but that was it for the day.

I took her back to the nursing home the next morning. She was tiring fast and the novelty was wearing off. As we zoomed up the M1 the effort of trying to shuffle words into some sort of order was too much for her and as a result I found my own sentences getting shorter and shorter until they almost vanished into thin air.

'Meadowhall.'

'Mmmm.'

I think she was glad to see the back of me. To be tucked up in her own bed and safe in her own mind where she wouldn't have to make the effort.

'*En-ig-ma.*'

Was it a one-off or did she understand more than we ever realized? And if so, had I ever discussed anything in her presence that would have hurt her? I tried not to think of that. God, I hope it never happens to me.

Aileen and I were both wrapped up in our own separate worlds as we drove away from the nursing home. She had known Goldie for a lot longer than I had and now she closed her eyes and dipped into the past.

'You all right?'

'Yes.'

I seem to have spent half my life moping around nursing homes and hospitals. It's like being on a roller coaster that is barely moving. The highs and lows come around at their own pace, the lows in the shape of misery, pain and humiliation; the highs in a sort of glory that makes life worth living.

I couldn't close my eyes – I was driving – but a couple of snapshots from the past came to life and mingled with the brake lights and the broken exhaust pipe of the car in front.

An aristocratic old lady sits up in bed, having her nails painted by a delightful young nurse who admires the birthday cards on her locker.

'Do you know how old you are today?'

The old lady considers the question for some time.

'I had it written down somewhere, but I've lost it. I must be all of seventy-six?'

The nurse dips a small brush into a bottle of clear varnish and gently takes hold of the woman's thin hand.

'You're a hundred and two.'

A warm smile crosses the old lady's face and she looks down on the pert little pony tail that is bobbing about under her nose.

'Don't be ridiculous, my child. Nobody lives to that age.'

Another time, another nurse – this one barely twenty. She stuffs a bedpan under the sheets and then lifts an old woman whose body seems to consist entirely of small bones sticking out through a covering of grey parchment.

'There you are, Doris.'

The woman's nightdress is open to the waist, exposing a thin flat breast straight out of the *National Geographic* magazine. I look away so as not to embarrass her, but she doesn't seem to know I am there. The nurse glances at her watch.

'You sit still, Doris. I won't be a minute.'

My eyes are drawn to her once more. She sits high on the bedpan, her back surprisingly straight as she stares after the retreating nurse. Then she murmurs softly to nobody in particular.

'My name is Mrs Rowley.'

I found the church hall by the usual method of driving around the outskirts of Leeds several times and then getting lucky. The television vans were parked on the street outside, and so I slipped into the small space between them and then slipped out again when they told me to bugger off.

One of the crew took pity on me and guided me to a spot right outside the front door where Aileen and I waited in a rather dismal porch for a break in the shooting.

This was a small, intimate film. The daily call sheet detailed the actors required for each scene. Pete and Thora – Pete and Gloria – Pete, Thora and Man – Pete, Thora, Margaret and Stunt Kitten.

More often than not the scenes would be two-handers, but today was the nearest thing we ever got to a remake of *Ben Hur*.

Along with Dame Thora we had Ruth Holden as Nellie Elliot and Dinah Handley as the Do-Gooder, together with a dozen whist-playing extras and a thousand Marks and Spencer's prawn and mayonnaise sandwiches playing themselves.

Or not as it turned out. This was a Granada/Yorkshire television production and at the time of shooting Marks and Spencer were suing Granada because of comments that had been made in a recent documentary, and there was no way Granada were going to give them free advertising time for their prawn and mayonnaise sandwiches. The props department had been busy producing a whole stack of fake labels that were to be stuck on to the Marks and Spencer packets, transforming them at a stroke into prawn and mayonnaise sandwiches made by the hitherto unknown firm of Field and Dunster.

The sandwiches took the switch in their stride and behaved like real professionals, glad of the chance to do a bit of proper acting for a change, but the packets weren't quite so versatile and remained absolute little sods to open.

'Cut.'

All over the room the whist players were struggling

with their triangles of plastic and cellophane, ripping the things to pieces, while at the main table Dinah Handley was having the devil's own job in her attempt to release Dame Thora's prawn sandwich into the wild.

Scouts were despatched to buy more supplies until there wasn't a prawn and mayonnaise sandwich left in the whole of Leeds and the Field and Dunster labels were running out fast.

'Action.'

'Damn it.'

'Cut.'

It wasn't until someone had the bright idea of easing back the little tags in advance that the scene began to take some sort of shape.

NELLIE (*to Do-Gooder*): They usually make 'em themselves, you know.

DO-GOODER: Maybe *they* do – but I had my Red Cross this morning and then there's the St John's Ambulance as soon as I've finished here. They're not cheap, you know.

MOTHER (*to Nellie*): What did she say they were?

DO-GOODER (*pouring tea*): They're prawn and mayonnaise.

MOTHER (*to Nellie*): You don't put prawns in a sandwich.

DO-GOODER: Field and Dunster do. They're very nice. Try it.

Deric's mother takes a tentative bite.

MOTHER: I've never been very keen on seafood myself. Apart from fish.

NELLIE: You eat crab. And we had that lobster in Blackpool.

MOTHER: And those.

NELLIE: You like cockles and mussels.

MOTHER: I like shrimps as well.

NELLIE: There you are then.

Deric's mother takes another bite, a more confident bite this time.

MOTHER (*to Do-Gooder*): It's very nice. Thank you. (*Confidentially*) It's just seafood I'm not so fond of.

Thora's timing of that last line was absolutely brilliant and I could sense the assembled company trying hard not to applaud.

'Cut.'

And then they applauded. All through the filming of the play Thora's timing had been an object lesson to any aspiring actor. We should have invited all the drama schools and charged admission.

'Action.'

This time Thora had to change the mood entirely. She took another bite of her sandwich, then reached out for her cup of tea. The cup swung loosely in her grip for a moment before slipping from her grasp. The camera closed in as she suffered her second stroke – in the background the extras looked on in horror.

MOTHER (*barely audible and unclear*): Jessie. (*Long pause*) Jessie.

This time there was no applause. It was far too real. This was something I had written, but had never witnessed. The details of my mother's stroke had come to me second hand and now it was happening before my eyes.

A couple of years ago Thora's husband Scotty had suffered the same fate while Thora was in another room and I wondered how she felt at this moment.

'Cut.'

She was helped into her wheelchair and brought over to where Aileen and I were propped against a table, surrounded by a regular army of prawn and mayonnaise sandwiches. She leaned over and pinched one, took a bite and then studied my face at close quarters.

'It hurts, doesn't it, love?'

After a pint in a local pub with Pete Postlethwaite, Aileen and I went over to Roundhay Park for a series of newspaper interviews with a band of journalists who had come all this way to talk to Thora and Pete, but who were prepared to put up with us in the meantime.

That afternoon we would be filming in a chemist's shop nearby and so a small corner of the park had been turned into what looked like a mobile holiday camp, with personal caravans for each of the leading actors, specialist trucks for make-up and wardrobe, and most essential of all, a couple of portable toilets with roller towels that actually worked.

There was a huge chuck wagon providing exceptionally good food in the circumstances and a single-decker bus cum dining car in which Aileen and I had been parked up at the far end.

I am not very good at showing off. I have always believed that the only compliments worth having are those that come from someone else, but today I was determined to let the journalists know that *Diana's Story* had recently been voted the most popular serial ever in the fifty-year history of the BBC's *Woman's Hour*. I was proud of the award. I had written the book and read the serial myself and so why not?

A journalist from a national paper plonked herself down on the other side of the table. She took out her

236

shorthand notebook and I took out my own trumpet and prepared to blow it.

'How's Thermal?'

'He's fine.'

'And Tigger?'

'She's very well.'

'I was very upset when Arthur died.'

'Yes, it was very sad.'

I put away my trumpet for the time being. From the other tables I could hear Penny talking about her previous work at the National Theatre. Pete was saying nice things about my script and Thora was starting from scratch with tales of her early days in provincial rep. And here was I – talking about my cats.

We discussed Frink's untimely death, which brought tears to the journalist's eyes, and then we moved on to the time when Thermal had been stoned out of his mind on home-made damson wine.

It was all very pleasant, but of course not a word would appear in the newspapers and I was determined to take the next interview by the scruff of the neck and point it in the right direction.

At a signal from the publicity people the journalists played musical chairs and this time we found ourselves in the company of the sort of man who wasn't about to take prisoners. He was tough and hard and jaded from years of show business interviews. He clicked a button on his portable tape recorder and leaned across the table, this time directing his questions at Aileen.

'How's Thermal?'

'He's fine.'

'And Tigger?'

'She's very well, thank you.'

*   *   *

We did have our moment of glory later on. In *Wide-Eyed and Legless* Aileen and I had walk-on parts as the guest speakers at a literary luncheon. The audience would have needed a pair of binoculars to spot us as we climbed on to a stage in the far distance, but as far as we are concerned it was the highlight of the film.

But there would be no chance of us doing a Hitchcock this time around. The scenes were too tight and too intimate and the last scene of all was being acted out right now, in the chemist's shop.

I peeped in through the window and watched as Pete and Malcolm Hebden ran through the two-handed exchange. There was hardly room enough to swing a packet of soluble aspirins and yet, as the two men eased themselves into the scene, all the necessary paraphernalia seemed to recede and then disappear.

The camera, the lights and the overhead microphone faded into the background, together with the spaghetti junction of wires and cables strewn across the floor. There is something sublime about watching two such excellent actors turn a couple of pages of script into a moment of real life.

And then it was all over. Thirty-one days of intensive graft and that was that. The film would now be edited and then join the rest of us in the long wait for transmission.

Out on the pavement Aileen and I had a smoke and a chat with Malcolm Hebden, who seemed like an old friend since he appeared in our kitchen several times a week, playing the part of Norris in *Coronation Street.*

David Whiteley, the sound recordist, had his box of tricks parked by the shop window as he checked through his script.

'Just the two answerphone voices to record back at the studio and we're finished.'

He glanced across at us.

'Why don't we get Deric and Aileen to do them while we're all set up?'

If I'd known I was to play the part of Colin on the answerphone I would have given him a damn sight more than four lines. I would have built the whole play around him. In every scene the phone would have rung at a crucial moment and there would have been Colin on the answerphone, a man of mystery.

And I certainly wouldn't have given Aileen twice as many lines as I had. Just for a moment I wondered if we might switch parts; but then common sense prevailed and after a quick rehearsal I had to admit that Aileen had been born to play the part of Mrs Bushell from the Guide Dogs.

We had about five minutes to rehearse. I could read from the script but of course Aileen had to learn every word off by heart, so we sat in the car while I read her part out loud to her in my best Mrs Bushell voice.

'Do it properly.'

'OK.'

She had it off pat in no time at all and we were ushered into the chemist's shop to put the final touches to the film. I cleared my throat and thought of the microphone as my friend.

'Aileen – it's Colin here . . .'

'Try it again.'

'Aileen – it's . . .'

'And once more.'

All in all I thought five takes was pretty good going. Colin is quite a complex character, even if he is only ringing Aileen to tell her that a spare part for her computer has now arrived, and I hope that my voice held the subtle hint of an unhappy childhood and a fairly healthy sex drive.

Aileen carried off her Mrs Bushell in a single take.

'That was brilliant, Aileen.'

Some you win and some you lose, but if I have my way that director will never work again.

Back at the studio they gave a small drinks party so that we could all say goodbye to one another. Thora had had the afternoon off and arrived looking every inch a Dame of the British Empire.

Aileen and I kept close to executive producer Keith Richardson. As usual he was smoking like a chimney and we were working on the theory that nobody was going to ask the boss if he would mind putting it out.

Dorothy Arnold was already there when we arrived. Without her wig and matching ensemble she looked nothing at all like the woman who had been Thora's double for the past thirty-one days. She had a photo album under her arm and she came across and shared it with us. The pictures traced her career in the music hall from way back and showed her wearing a series of rather racy frocks or, more often than not, nothing more than a fan and a couple of tassels. On some she was without the tassels and hadn't quite been quick enough with the fan.

After a while she sat down with Thora and together they thumbed through the album. I wondered what Thora would make of it. She is known for her dislike of bad language and sex on television and remembered fondly as the presenter of *Songs of Praise.*

Page after page went slowly by and then finally Thora handed the album back.

'Well there's one thing certain, love, they are never going to ask me to double for you.'

Wish I had written that.

Chapter Eighteen

The film was due to be televised in October and Transworld had re-jacketed the paperback of *Lost for Words* to coincide with the transmission date.

When the book was first published the cover sported a photograph of me and my mother, which was then replaced by one of Jim Broadbent and Thora Hird when *Wide-Eyed and Legless* was televised.

Now the cover took on yet another life with a photograph of Pete and Thora sitting at my mother's kitchen table. By now the poor book must have been as confused as those Marks and Spencer's prawn and mayonnaise sandwiches over in Leeds.

Then the powers that be decided to hold the film back until Christmas, hoping for a larger audience, and bookshop customers all over the country must have been as confused as the sandwiches and the book itself when they read that *Lost for Words* was now a major television film.

'Don't ever remember seeing that.'

It turned out to be rather a smart move. We sold out long before Christmas and the book had to be reprinted.

*   *   *

Meantime back in Huddersfield life continued much as before. Aileen had been buying suitable Christmas presents throughout the year and now she couldn't remember where on earth she had put them. Apparently many of these suitable presents were from me to her, so I wasn't allowed to help her look for them.

'Surely if I'm supposed to have bought them for you, then it won't matter if I know what they are?'

'It'll spoil the surprise.'

I knew there was something wrong with that but I couldn't for the life of me think what it was, so she put my mind at rest.

'It'll be more fun if you find out on the day.'

Of course. That was it. Sometimes I'm a bit slow on the uptake.

At least I'm allowed to do all the Christmas shopping, write over three hundred Christmas cards and put up all the decorations, so don't anybody go thinking I'm henpecked.

In fact I am really rather well organized these days and I had it all done and dusted at least ten days before Christmas. All, that is, except for a few bits and pieces in the dining room, a touch of tinsel here, a little holly there, and I was sorting them out on my hands and knees when Thermal came running into the room.

'*Little Chap's back.*'

'Where is he?'

'*He's unconscious in the cellar.*'

I followed Thermal down the cellar steps and wondered what sort of condition our occasional cat would be in this time. You can only go on burning the candle at both ends for so long and by now Little Chap must have just about the shortest wick in Huddersfield.

At least he had made it as far as his basket. His front end was all tucked up neatly, his head resting on the cheap tartan car rug that the cats had taken over after it had shrunk in the wash and almost disappeared.

But his rear end hadn't been quite so lucky. It looked as though someone had thrown him at the basket from a great distance and missed, and his haunches sprawled half in and half out, his two hind legs spreadeagled across the central heating boiler.

For the umpteenth time my heart fell and I wondered if he had been in some sort of accident, but as I tried to tuck his rear end gently into the basket he started, then quickly scrambled to his feet and threw back his head.

'*Fooo-oood.*'

He'd been gone for quite a while and we were happy to have him back again. After he had downed a couple of saucers full of nourishing Whiskas and another half-full of semi-skimmed milk, he joined me among the baubles on the dining-room floor and immediately took a large chunk out of Frosty the Snowman's head.

'That wasn't very nice.'

Frosty and I have been together now for some thirty-five years and I had promised him that this year he could stand under the flowering cactus in the window and be a special feature.

But he didn't look quite the same now. He tried to smile but it doesn't come easily when a cat has just bitten off half your face, and I could tell that he was disappointed. So I still stuck him under the cactus, but turned him round with his back to us so that he was staring out of the window.

'Now we can see your sack properly.'

He didn't say anything, but he's not daft.

*   *   *

Little Chap's social skills still require a lot of work. He gave a passing thump to a recently retired fairy and then went and sat under the dining table and began to scratch all those parts that even a Russian gymnast would have had trouble in reaching.

Whenever he returns from one of his journeys into the unknown he brings with him a whole lorryload of fleas and he seems quite happy to have them aboard.

'A flea isn't just for Christmas, you know – it's for life.'

The others sit and stare in amazement as he bites and scratches, furks and gouges. This is his hobby, this is what he is good at, and over the years he has turned himself into a master craftsman.

Nevertheless I can't be doing with it under my dining table and I was just about to sort him out when Aileen appeared wearing her satin robe and a half-baked expression.

'Little Chap's back,' I told her.

'I know. I could hear him scratching. He woke me up.'

I made her a cup of tea and poured a drop in a saucer for Thermal. He took a delicate sip and then frowned.

'You've forgotten the sweetener.'

Aileen took a sip from her cup and grimaced.

'I know. I've forgotten the sweetener.'

But I hadn't forgotten about Little Chap. I usually manage to get hold of him as soon as he thumps in through the cat flap. He's the only one who will have anything to do with the flea powder. The others run a mile. Thermal even takes off first thing every morning, the minute I pick up a can of deodorant. They have been spoilt rotten. They prefer to go private, demanding either a little drop of Tiguvon on the back of the neck or a small dash of Program as part of a calorie-controlled diet.

Little Chap isn't as fussy, mainly because he has no idea what is going on and his ignorance has enabled me to clear out most of the cans of old flea powder from the back of the cupboard. If I brush him for a moment or two he disappears into a world of his own – his mouth falls wide open and his body relaxes to such an extent that at any moment I almost expect one of his legs to drop off.

At this point I reach out for the can of flea powder and the other cats take cover behind the sideboard, doing their best to warn him of the oncoming danger.

'*Look out! He's behind you.*'

But a little scrub at the base of his tail will make sure that Little Chap stays safely tucked away in Never-Never Land and before long I can hear the fleas coughing and spluttering.

'*My chest feels just like sandpaper.*'

'*There's a lot of it going about.*'

But this time the hole in the canister was all bunged up and so I had to improvise. I massaged Little Chap with my knee while I poked the hole free with the thin wire stalk of a Christmas tree bauble. It took a bit of doing but in the end it worked a treat, so I gave him a practice squirt and then sat back on my heels to admire my handiwork.

He had a broad white line right down the length of his back and his tail. One moment I was dealing with an affectionate, albeit flea-ridden, moggie and the next I was the proud owner of a small but beautifully marked skunk.

He couldn't believe it. He stood up, took one look at himself and sat down again.

'*What on earth have you done?*'

Well, how can you explain to a cat that you have just sprayed him with a can full of artificial snow?

I couldn't believe I could have been so stupid. I made a grab for him so that I could put matters right, but he was off down the cellar and out through the cat flap before you could say Jack Frost.

It didn't take long to find him. We don't have all that many skunks in Huddersfield and Sarah, my neighbour, was surprised to see one sitting on her kitchen window sill.

The good thing about Little Chap is that he doesn't bear a grudge and I'm sure he will forgive me eventually. I'm not so sure about the small herd of albino fleas who were unfortunately caught in the crossfire.

Sarah pushed him under the hedge to me and I caught him on my side as he came up for air. Sarah peered through the hedge to see if all was well.

'Have you got him?'

I hoisted Little Chap up on my shoulder. He looked ridiculous.

'Yes, thank you.'

'Good. I'll go and get on with my Christmas decorations. Have you finished yours yet?'

'Not quite,' I told her. 'But I've made a start.'

That afternoon I went out to buy a copy of the *Radio Times*. Ever since I can remember the Christmas double issue has been one of the highlights of the festive season. As a teenager I would pounce on it the moment it dropped through the letter box and work out a programme of things not to be missed.

This time I bought the *TV Times* as well and took them both for a cup of coffee and a toasted teacake.

I think they enjoyed it, but for me it was something of a disappointment. I went straight to 23 December, hoping to see photographs of Thora and Pete and maybe a few kind words, but we weren't even listed.

I shuffled through the other thirteen days to see if we had been moved sideways for some reason, but nowhere was there any mention of *Lost for Words.*

The coffee had gone cold and the toasted teacake had lost all confidence in itself and become listless and morose. Even the two magazines seemed to suspect there was something wrong, so I tried to cheer them up.

'Must be some good reason for it, I suppose.'

But my heart wasn't in it. I had added a note to all my Christmas cards – '*Lost for Words*, 23rd Dec. ITV' – and now I looked like an idiot.

I took the two magazines home with me, but left the coffee and the teacake sitting miserably on the restaurant table. I could feel their eyes boring into the back of my neck as I pushed open the door, but thought it best not to look round.

The 'good reason' came later that afternoon in a phone call from Keith Richardson and it was quickly followed by a call from Sally, who wanted to know what on earth had happened.

'You're not listed anywhere.'

'No, I know. The people down at the network found that we would have been scheduled right opposite Dame Judi Dench and Billy Connolly in *Mrs Brown* on BBC1, so now we're going out on January the third.'

For the next half hour or so we had one of those talks. You know the sort – one of those talks when somebody who loves you very much takes logic by the scruff of the neck, bends it in half, and then goes searching for all the reasons why what has just happened is really for the best.

'Lots of people would be going out to parties that night.'

'That's true.'

'By the third of January they'll have had enough and they'll want to put their feet up and stay in and watch television.'

'Yes, that's very true.'

'I think it's brilliant news really.'

What was really brilliant was having a daughter like Sally, especially when she told me about her Christmas present for Steve. She'd wanted it to be a big surprise.

'So I bought him a load of weightlifting equipment. One of those bars with a huge selection of weights that you screw on either end. I wanted it to be a big surprise, so I asked them if they would mind gift-wrapping it for me so that he wouldn't know what it was and they said they would be delighted to and it took them ages and they made a really good job of it. But then I tried to pick it up and I couldn't even lift it off the counter and I realized that there was no way I was going to get it home on the bus.'

So Steve had to go into Brighton and fetch it himself. She's a lovely girl. She's a lot like me.

Christmas was going to be a quiet affair. Aileen's daughter Annie was coming up from London with her brother David and we were going to laze about and do as little as possible.

Our doctor, Helen, had invited us to one of her wonderful parties that go on and on for ever and we were really looking forward to that – until her husband John rang and told us it was off.

'Is there anything wrong?'

'No. We just can't be bothered.'

I think that's wonderful. I would have invented some complicated story that involved Aileen having contracted a mysterious and highly contagious disease that required her to lie in a darkened room over the Christmas period.

I would be ever so sorry and hope that it hadn't screwed up everyone's plans over the festive season and Aileen would be furious with me and then have to spend the next couple of months explaining her miraculous recovery to all and sundry.

But John and Helen just couldn't be bothered and everyone understood. I have a lot to learn.

As 3 January crept ever closer a number of previews began to appear in the national newspapers. Without exception they were encouraging to say the least.

. . . but you will have to wait until after Christmas for what is arguably the pick of the crop on any channel, ITV's Lost for Words. *The schedulers ummed and aahed about where to put this little gem, and eventually settled for a post-hangover slot, January 3.* That was the *Sunday Times.*

I didn't let it go to my head of course. I merely glanced at the article and then put it aside, then picked it up and merely glanced at it once more while I was in the bath and then again later, sitting on the toilet. I merely glanced at it as I washed the pots, before taking the paper out with me into the garden, spreading it out on the paving stones so that I could glance at it every now and then as I weeded the rockery.

Nick rang a little later.

'Have you seen that wonderful piece in the *Sunday Times*?'

'I glanced at it.'

I have lost count of the number of writers, directors and actors who say that they never ever read their reviews, and just maybe, tucked away among that formidable army, there might be the odd one or two who are actually telling the truth.

But reviews matter to me. I want people to like what I have done, and I was increasingly delighted as both the tabloids and the broadsheets joined together in singing our praises, giving rave reviews to Dame Thora and Pete.

I already had a video of the film, but watching your work go out live always adds an extra edge. So on 3 January we settled down early with *Coronation Street* and mourned the passing of Alf Roberts along with eighteen million other like-minded souls.

We put Chris Tarrant on mute for half an hour, which I always think is for the best, and worked our way through the *Daily Telegraph* crossword until he had stopped being silly and gone home.

For once I wouldn't have to talk Aileen through the scenery, the action and the quiet bits, she knew it backwards. So we snuggled up on the settee in her study and for the first time in my life I sat and enjoyed the adverts.

No one had told me that the play was to be sponsored by HSBC Midland Bank in their Great British Drama series. My mind went back to all those Friday mornings long ago, when I would hang around the front door of their Chesterfield branch, waiting to cash a cheque to pay the wages, trying to spot a cashier who didn't know me and who would be less likely to say that the manager would like a word with me in his office.

The Midland were very patient with me. They could have pulled the rug out from underneath my feet at any time, but they gave me a lot of rope and eventually we finished up all square. Then a few years ago they invited Aileen and me to cut a ribbon and declare open the refurbished branch of the Midland Bank up here in Marsh, and now here they were providing the wrap-around commercial for the play. It's what they call a happy ending.

Which is hardly what we had in the play. As it drew to an end I could barely see the screen for tears. Thora and my mother have become inextricably linked in my mind over the past few years, through two films and many happy times together, and as her hand moved slowly across the bedspread and covered Pete's it was as though I was losing both of them at once.

Sometimes when I think of my mother I see her with Thora's face and have to fish out some old photographs, and even then it's hard to separate the two. They have almost merged and become one. Not long ago I found a note I made many years ago after calling in to see my mother, just after my father had died.

She was sorting through some leaflets from the DHSS.

'I'm a single parent now.'

Her eyes lit up at the thought of an extra allowance.

'I don't think they'll wear it, Mum.'

'You don't?'

'No. Not when your son is in his early forties and married with two kids.'

As I ran the moment over in my mind I could see my mother's lovely and ever hopeful face, and yet the words came through loud and clear in Dame Thora's voice.

Or was it the other way around? I don't suppose it matters. The two of them are locked together in my memory for ever and they couldn't be in better company.

*   *   *

The next morning I bought all the papers and read the reviews and we couldn't have done a better job if we had written them ourselves. Thora and Pete received a whole bunch of rave notices and there was even the odd pat on the back for the writer. Teletext carried seven pages of viewers' comments, all of them singing our praises. And then the news came through that we had captured an audience of over twelve million and I sat down and tried to imagine what twelve million people would look like if they were all bundled together in one place. The best I could do was to close my eyes and imagine Wembley Stadium on Cup Final day, and then multiply it by one hundred and sixty.

Of course there's always one, and this time it was Robert Hanks in the *Independent*. He didn't like the play at all and he ended his review with a rather smart-arsed comment that must have seemed awfully clever at the time.

'. . . *this was as cheerful and life-enhancing as rouge on a corpse's cheeks.*'

A little over the top, I thought, and just a mite clumsy. I would have written, '. . . *as rouge on the cheeks of a corpse.*'

But then he was probably in a hurry to meet a dead-line at the time and heaven forbid that anyone should think I can't take a bit of criticism. If he didn't like the play then he had every right to pan it. That's what he is paid for and if ever we should meet I shall tell him so. I shall give him a broad smile and shake him by the hand and then bring my right knee up sharply into his groin.

Postscript

Whenever I have a bout of the flu my mind drifts sideways into a fantasy world. My son-in-law Steve has the same problem. He worries about broccoli.

I worried about the bedside rug. It seemed frightened. All alone and vulnerable on the bedroom floor, it trembled slightly, its pile standing on end, and so I rolled it up and hid it in the bottom of the wardrobe where it would be safe from its many predators, any of whom can turn the life of a bedside rug into a living nightmare.

As I struggled back between the damp sheets my head swam and my body quickly heated itself back up to the two hundred degrees centigrade at which I had simmered gently for the past few days.

My chest pounded, as did the small white cat who happened to be sitting on it at the time.

'Stop it, Thermal.'

Later Aileen brought me a cup of tea and the evening paper, then settled herself on the side of the bed.

'I think you're sitting on Tigger, love.'

'Sorry.'

A rather flat tortoiseshell cat crawled up from between the sheets and laid her head on the pillow beside me.

'Are you all right?'

'*Just give me a minute.*'

Aileen stroked her better.

'Are they all here?'

'Three of them. Thermal's asleep on my chest and William is in charge of my genitalia.'

But as soon as Aileen left the room all three of them followed her. It was time for their dinner and dinner can be a most exciting meal when Aileen is in charge. She is never quite sure which tin she is opening and her offerings over the years have ranged from Whiskas tuna and chicken to Del Monte's pineapple chunks in syrup.

I sat up and drank my tea, thumbing through the *Huddersfield Examiner* until I found the Denis Kilcommons column. He's a good man, is Denis. Once wrote a cracking thriller called *The Dark Apostle* and today he was writing about me.

Apparently the video of *Lost for Words* had just been released. Denis knew all about it, which is more than I did. I picked up the phone and rang Nick in Stratford.

After a long conversation with a woman in Bridgnorth who told me to keep well wrapped up and take plenty of liquids I had another go at ringing Nick, this time dialling a number which bore a much closer resemblance to his.

As I waited for him to answer the phone I couldn't help thinking how pleasant the woman in Bridgnorth had been, especially since her husband had just left her for a girl half her age and now she'd broken out in this rash.

*   *   *

Nick was really excited about the video and promised to comb the shops in Stratford first thing in the morning to see if they had it in stock.

'Only I can't get out of bed at the moment and it would be nice to know.'

'You leave it to me.'

I have nice kids. He also told me to stay well wrapped up and to take lots of liquids.

The next morning the fever had gone and all was well with the world. The little bird on the roof had woken me at just before six with a brand new reggae version of 'Lady Madonna' and I lay in bed and listened with a wonderfully clear head to his entire repertoire before sadly coming to the conclusion that he was tone deaf.

I dozed on and off for the next three hours, not wanting to move in case I set him off again. Then the phone rang. It was Nick on his mobile.

'Hi, Dad. I've been to W. H. Smith's and they've got a shelf full and now I'm outside Our Price. They had five and they've sold four, so I bought the last one.'

'Oh, that's terrific.'

He hesitated.

'Just one thing. They haven't put your name on the cover, just Thora's and Pete's.'

I reached out for the *Examiner*.

'They have. There's a photo of it in the paper. It says *by Deric Longden*. Up near the top right-hand corner.'

He hesitated again.

'Just a minute.'

I heard a short spell of heavy breathing as he tucked the phone under his chin, and then a scratching sound before he came back on the line.

'You're right. They'd stuck the price ticket over it.'

I told you I was famous.